Praise for

The Living Maya

"Robert Sitler, anguished by our destruction of the environment and civil life, opens *The Living Maya* with an analysis of the prophecies and predictions around 2012. The very people, who had the astronomical genius to base a calendar on the coming alignment in the rift of the Milky Way, transmit through their way of life, the seeds for our desperately needed personal and cultural transformation. Sitler documents the values and relationships that sustain the Maya and that can sustain us. We walk the 'road' with him so we also might live in vital relationship with the earth, be in true and vibrant community with each other, birth and raise skillful and wise children, and be guided again by the great hearts of the spirits."

—DEENA METZGER, author of *Writing for Your Life; Ruin and Beauty: New and Selected Poems; Tree: Essays and Pieces;* and *Entering the Ghost River: Meditations on the Theory and Practice of Healing*

"This lucid book by a long-time scholar of the Mayan people provides the reader with a rich cultural context against which to weigh the deeper significance of the 2012 phenomenon. Robert Sitler's approach is balanced, informed, heartfelt, and profoundly respectful of the wisdom of Mayan traditions."

—PHILLIP LUCAS, PhD, founding editor of *Nova Religio: The Journal of Alternative and Emergent Religions;* professor of religious studies, Stetson University, DeLand, Florida; and author of *New Religious Movements in the Twenty-First Century: Legal, Political, and Social Challenges in Global Perspective*

"This extraordinary narrative, told by a scholar with many years of experience among the Mayan people, is a path of heart into their worlds, both ancient and modern. At a time when the global New Age and academic communities are stalemated in disagreement over what significance lies in the upcoming December 21, 2012 date, this book steps gently and boldly into that radical middle ground and informs us of the living Mayas' message to us. Anyone who acknowledges that our crumbling family cohesiveness and fast-paced urban lifestyles are toxic and alienating should pay attention to this message. It doesn't come from other planets or galaxies, or from some other dimension, nor even from some esoteric mysteries that the ancient priests possessed. It arises from the Maya who have had—in spite of conquest and oppression—many generations of connectedness to their land and their sacred shrines. It arises from their ritual observances, their daily rounds which honor the ancestors, the newborn babies and the family, the rains and winds, and the newly-planted seeds. It is another universe of human potential, but one which, if we pay attention, helps us to listen to our own heartbeat."

—BARBARA MACLEOD, PHD, independent scholar and author of
An Epigrapher's Annotated Index to Cholan and Yucatecan Verb Morphology

"*The Living Maya* is a remarkable exploration of the significance of 2012 that is both introspective and open-minded, by a scholar who has, unlike most authors on the subject, spent considerable time among the modern Maya.... The book describes the profoundly practical worldview of the Maya, which has enabled them to survive war and catastrophe and may contain the wisdom we need to survive as a species."

—MATTHEW LOOPER, PHD, professor of art,
California State University, Chico

The Living Maya

Ancient Wisdom
in the Era of **2012**

Robert K. Sitler, PhD

North Atlantic Books
Berkeley, California

Published by North Atlantic Books
P.O. Box 12327
Berkeley, California 94712

Cover art *Veneración al dios del maíz* by Mario Gonzalez Chavajay, 2008
Cover and book design by Susan Quasha
Printed in the United States of America

The Living Maya: Ancient Wisdom in the Era of 2012 is sponsored by the Society for the Study of Native Arts and Sciences, a nonprofit educational corporation whose goals are to develop an educational and cross-cultural perspective linking various scientific, social, and artistic fields; to nurture a holistic view of arts, sciences, humanities, and healing; and to publish and distribute literature on the relationship of mind, body, and nature.

North Atlantic Books' publications are available through most bookstores. For further information, visit our website at www.northatlanticbooks.com or call 800-733-3000.

Library of Congress Cataloging-in-Publication Data
Sitler, Robert, 1955–
 The living Maya: ancient wisdom in the era of 2012 / Robert Sitler.
   p. cm.
 Includes bibliographical references.
 ISBN 978-1-55643-939-1
  1. Mayas—Social life and customs. 2. Maya philosophy. 3. Social values. 4. Wisdom. 5. Two thousand twelve, A.D. 6. Social problems. 7. Civilization, Modern—21st century. 8. Sitler, Robert, 1955–. 9. Travel—Central America. I. Title.
 F14353.S7S58 2010
 305.897'42—dc22
              2010000619

1 2 3 4 5 6 7 8 9 MALLOY 14 13 12 11 10

To my beloved June,
Goddess manifest

Acknowledgments to the Living Maya

Chhonta chey.[1] *Mal tyox. K'ak'namal. K'u bo'otik. Wokolawal. Yuh wal dyos. Kolaval. Wokolix awalo. Ban tyox. Dyos bo'otik.*

I offer my thanks in just a few of your more than two dozen languages. Numerous kindhearted souls among you and your remarkably diverse cultural traditions have inspired my life. Even so, I have no ability nor inclination to speak on your behalf. This book attempts to convey what are merely my own reflections on time spent in your communities and inevitably reveals far more about me than it tells about your world. I ask your pardon in advance for shortcomings in my perceptual capacities. Like the first true human beings modeled from corn dough by the primordial spirits in the holy *Popol Vuh,* I see through eyes deliberately and mercifully clouded by our creators.

Contents

Foreword

We begin with the premise that the human species living in different parts of planet Earth is all one. Everything that occurs on this ship that we're traveling upon through space and time concerns us all. The destiny of our beautiful and privileged planet, home to more than six billion human beings, is unknown to us. Thus far, to our limited knowledge, it is the only space in the universe where the necessary conditions exist for life. The human being and other living creatures enter into the cyclical process of birth, growth, reproduction, and death—transformation as a natural law of existence. That's probably also the case for stars and our Earth since they someday too will cease to exist.

The differences between human beings lie in their cultural expressions; in terms of biology, all humans are similar with only small variations. But those cultural differences—which can be summarized as forms of conceiving, processing, and communicating the world and life—exercise great influence on human actions. Many times large conflicts between one group and another arise due to these differences.

In the beginning, as human groups became conscious of their existence on the face of the Earth, huge questions arose concerning the causes and effects of natural and social phenomena, about where we came from, our origins, and our final destiny. We asked about what there is in the physical realm, what there is beyond the physical, and the transcendental. In this way, cultures and civilizations were constructed. We also fixed our attention on the Earth and what might lie beyond her to form concepts, relationships, and meanings.

History records early periods in human evolution that gave way to other stages in which the bases of civilizations were laid down. One of these civilizations was that of the Maya, who were called skywatchers by one author because they fixed their gaze on the stars and their movement across time. The study of time was their obsession and through it they created complex mathematical systems based on elements in life, such as the zero as a seed that germinates into ideas and existence; their twenty-based numbering derived from the ten fingers and ten toes a person *(winaq)* has; and the number thirteen that indicates the thirteen Mayan months of human gestation and the thirteen articulations of the human body. The complex Mayan numerical system was built with only three elements—the zero, a dot, and a line—while other cultures need to use a larger quantity of elements.

Many say that the Maya disappeared. This is not the truth since in the Mesoamerican area there currently exist more than six million Maya practicing the elements of their ancient culture such as religion, languages, numbering, and medicine based on natural products, arts, and the calendar that is one of the most important legacies of this people.

Regarding the calendars utilized by the Maya one finds the *tzolkin*, the *haab*, the *tun*, the *k'atun*, and the *baktun*. The *baktun* counts the eras of creation. The thirteenth of the *baktuns* is nearing its end on the 21st of December in 2012. This is considered to be the era of the Men of Corn and it had its beginning over three thousand years before the Christian era.

One of those currently studying Mayan culture is Professor Robert Sitler, Director of Latin American Studies at Stetson University in Florida. Dr. Sitler has been visiting for many years in Guatemala and Mexico, specifically to a remote Mayan community of Mam-speakers set in a valley with surrounding peaks of nearly twelve thousand feet in the Cuchumatán Mountains. Mam is one of the thirty Mayan languages currently spoken in Mesoamerica, and its speakers are mostly traditional people who maintain the customs of their ancestors including the language, hand-woven clothing, and religious elements.

From his first visits among the Mam, Dr. Sitler opted for sharing life with this ancient community, leaving behind the comforts of life in the United States. He experienced the community's religion and spirituality, learned to speak some of its language, ate its food, lived its values, and shared distinctive moments in that town of the culture of corn. In the steep slopes of the Cuchumatanes, the highest mountains in Central America, one can breathe the peaceful air amid the firs, cypress, and pines while watching herds of sheep grazing up on the high plains. In this world apart from the noises of the city and modernity, Dr. Sitler soon became deserving of the friendship and kindness of many types of people of all ages in Todos Santos. Going down the streets of town one can hear people saying *"Adiós, tat Roberto,"* an honorific greeting earned through service and camaraderie.

Through his visits there he observed and learned ancestral knowledge, practicing the lifestyles and customs of the Todosanteros with simplicity and humility. Dr. Sitler has not only researched Mayan culture from the academy and its libraries, but he has had practical experience with those elements of the living culture. This book, appropriately called *The Living Maya,* can convey important information to us accurately thanks to the life experiences he has collected and narrated here.

Among those important messages, the author speaks to us of Mayan childrearing methods used in which children learn to live in nature with harmony and respect: Father Sun, Mother Moon, Mother Corn, the animal and plant brothers and sisters. We share spaces with nature, and the *ahaws* (lords) have only lent them to us. By caring for nature and the environment, we guarantee our own existence and well-being. But Mother Earth only gives us what is necessary for human life.

Since long ago, the ancient Maya predicted the end of the present era as the end of a cycle in their calendar. In life everything is cyclical; everything ends and gives birth to a new stage. In this sense, humanity should take up its responsibility to care for planet Earth. The social and communal fabric is made from the practice of values and the building of peace, with each individual fulfilling the norms of common law that have operated in the communities for many centuries.

Another cultural aspect the author communicates to us in his book is that the Maya value the knowledge and honor the experiences and wisdom of the ancients, the elders and ancestors. Knowledge is accumulative and nothing is rejected. These beliefs and values are carried into practice and not just left in the realm of ideologies.

Through his work, Dr. Sitler carries the teachings of a millennial culture to the world, wisdom that can be useful in helping humanity take into account its responsibilities for the care of its home planet Earth. Motivated by the arrival of 2012, upon finishing the present era of the Men of Corn, we are all called to reflect upon our destiny and listen to the words of Professor Sitler and the voices of the Maya.

Swatx'ilal hek'ul (Peace in your hearts)

Kaxhin (Q'anhobal Maya)

GASPAR PEDRO GONZÁLEZ
author of *13 Baktun: Mayan Visions of 2012 and Beyond*

Foreword

December 21, 2012, would have been just another day and yet another year for the contemporary Maya. It may not be so anymore.

Hyped foreign interest now claims the date found carved on a monument at the archaeological site of Tortuguero in Tabasco, Mexico, is shrouded in mystery. Scholars have set off a flurry of theories linked to natural occurrences, like the movement of the planets, solar flares, environmental change, the celebration of creation, and the tilting of Earth on its axis. Some have stretched the truth and entrapped the gullible into believing the Maya said the date marks the end of the world.

There are certain truths that surround the Mayan date marking the end of a cycle in the Long Count calendar of the ancient Maya. The Maya did carve the date on a stone monument. They also recorded an event telling us about the date. And nature, in its infinite power, has left us contemporary Maya and Mayanists guessing. Nature eroded whatever corresponding data the Maya left and we don't know what the date means.

It leads to one obvious fact: the Maya did not say an apocalypse will occur on that date.

The date hangs as an open note in time and those with creative imaginations have jumped at the opportunity to create theories about the date, including one that we will cease to exist on December 21, 2012, feeding on the fear of those who are less knowledgeable. The non-Mayan ideas derive from people who might have read about the Maya, people who have dug up the bones and artifacts of the ancient Maya in their quest to understand a sophisticated civilization with many elements that have eluded us, or people who realized anything Mayan is potentially marketable.

To the contemporary Maya, changes in the environment, constantly moving planets, the celebration of creation and rebirth, are not new. Mayas still hold on to the tradition of respecting the earth, using heavenly bodies to guide their use of the soil. They maintain their simple form of calendar and believe everything around us has life. Maya are aware of the changes that occur at the end of every *haab*, a yearlong cycle, and every year after that. So, 2012 would be just another year in the life of a Mayan farmer toiling in the fields hoping his observation of the stars and weather would help him maximize his yield of food to keep his family and way of life alive.

To a large extent, most of the 2012 theorists, far removed from the realities, customs, and traditions the Maya inherited from the ancestors, have neglected to include the view of the contemporary Maya. They have failed to include the Maya in their discussions of what they claim is Mayan.

In his book *The Living Maya*, Robert Sitler seeks out the contemporary Mayan perspective to assist his research in explaining the 2012 phenomenon. He weaves a story of his personal experiences with the wisdom of Mayan priests, elders, and the ordinary Mayan people he met along his way as he traveled the Mayan world. Professor Sitler's book gives us a glimpse of Mayan thought, largely discounted by Mayanists as uneducated and whose contributions to intellectual conversations are constantly dismissed as mythical lore.

He goes beyond the parameters of archaeological digs to see how much of what is found on centuries-old hieroglyphs still thrives in Mayan society and how it ties to 2012. *The Living Maya* explores the traditions, customs, and spirituality of contemporary Maya in communities in the highlands of Guatemala and in villages in Yucatán, Mexico, and Belize. Professor Sitler's quest to understand the Maya has put him in contact with a people thought to be extinct. Rather than stand on the outside looking in, he takes the initiative to spend time in Mayan villages, living their lifestyle to better understand a simple existence that thrives on respect. For instance, in his book, the author is puzzled about an elderly man sleeping on the street with people walking around. Respect for an elder is primary in Mayan communities and the fact that everyone lets the sleeping old man rest in the street does not mean he is not protected if he needs to be.

Foreword

Professor Sitler writes with knowledge afforded to him by his travels in the Mayan countryside. He speaks eloquently of weaving, of the birthing process, of respect of the elders, of experiencing the spiritual, and of honoring nature. The ability to do so is enhanced by his willingness to be a part of remote communities and because the book *The Living Maya* is inclusive of the Mayan perspective.

To achieve the goal of completing his book, Professor Sitler has been willing to entrust his life to the hands of an unknown Mayan medicine woman, who performed suction acupuncture on his back. Blood flowed as the sharp stingray spines pierced his skin and the Mayan woman lit an oil-soaked piece of cotton inside a glass and applied it to his back to draw out the bad blood. He trekked in ankle-deep mud on a trail visible only to the native Maya, who through familiarity with the land know where the paths are. And after hours of walking in mud and rain, he unhesitatingly fell to his stomach and crawled into a hole barely large enough to let a grown man through to explore an underground cave, once used as a dwelling by the ancient Maya. And in the light of oil lamps, he danced to melodic tunes of a Mayan harp, joining village women and men as they enjoyed a pastime that possibly dates back hundreds of years.

There is no doubt that by the onset of December 21, 2012, the latest invasion—foreign misinformation—will hit Mayan communities. And like the plagues that afflicted us with the arrival of the Dzulo'ob[1] many centuries ago, this new phenomenon will create anxiety and fear in our people. But the strength and wisdom of elders will surge again, to show us the natural way, in which we have learned to embrace all that has caused us discomfort and overcome it. In a similar way, *The Living Maya*, which focuses on the simplicity of Mayan life, can orient us to the adjustments we may need to make after our brush with a different perspective on 2012.

PATRICIO BALONA (YUKATEK MAYA)
Reporter for *The Daytona Beach News-Journal*, and nephew and student of Don Elijio Pantí, renowned Mayan healer from San Antonio, Cayo District, Belize

CHAPTER 1

Clearing the Road to 2012

A selection of just a few of the recent books on 2012.

First Steps

Maya[1] frequently use the image of a path or road as a metaphor for human life. For example, when rural Yukatek Maya ask, *"Bix a bel?"* ("How is your road?"), they are not merely inquiring about current trail conditions, a practical consideration for people who still sometimes travel great distances on foot; they are also asking about your present state of being as you walk. The eighty thousand Q'anhobal Maya who live in the high-altitude valleys of the Cuchumatán Mountains of northwest Guatemala use the road metaphor

with a slightly different twist. There, the title for one of their revered
spiritual guides is *ahbe'*, or "person of the road," a being assumed to
have attained a heightened capacity to provide reliable direction for
one's life journey by virtue of his or her own lengthy experience walking literal and figurative roads. The living Maya continue a collective ancestral journey on a cultural path already some three thousand
years in length. Their culture's well-worn road has already taken them
through extreme challenges including near societal collapse, mass die-
offs due to pandemic diseases, and even barbarically violent attempts
by outsiders to vanquish the Maya and their traditions. Maya have
acquired their millennial knowledge concerning the human journey
through repeated periods of severe hardship and more than a hundred generations of human experience. As the much-heralded year
2012 approaches, the experientially acquired wisdom of this ancient
culture offers us time-proven guidance based upon the Maya's profound familiarity with the twists and turns on life's many roads.

In these pages I intend to share my own perception of Mayan
ways, personal perspectives derived from my own walks on hundreds
of trails in Guatemala, Mexico, and Belize over the past thirty-plus
years among people speaking more than a dozen Mayan languages.
As I proceed in this book, I utilize this experiential grounding in Mayan culture for direction in coming to terms with the multifaceted and
sometimes bewildering topic of 2012[2] and the Mayan calendar. Just as
when hiking on narrow Mayan footpaths in an unfamiliar area, when
trying to communicate about radically different cultural traditions
such as those of the Maya and to explore the potential esoteric significance of their ancient calendars, it is helpful for the trail ahead to be
clear of obstructions. For that reason, I begin the book by describing
a bit of my own life journey, including some of its curious detours;
the first lessons learned while hiking Mayan trails with my wife in
Mexico; and my gradual development of a better informed and multivalent appreciation for the potential significance of the year 2012. I
write about myself, not because my personal saga is of any inordinate
importance, but merely so readers have a clearer sense of "where I'm

coming from" and thus can more easily assess my value as a guide. I hope to remove as many impediments as I can from our road to a richer understanding of the world of the living Maya, its elaborate calendar systems, and the portentous year 2012 itself.

Approaching fruition of the thirteenth *pik* (pronounced "peek") cycle in the ancient Long Count calendar during the highly anticipated year 2012, some of my fellow New Agers describe the Maya as highly evolved spiritual messengers from a distant constellation. These extra-terrestrial Maya come, it is said, to guide an increasingly disoriented humanity at this time of unprecedented socio-environmental crisis. I agree wholeheartedly that Mayan ways have much to offer us at this uniquely critical juncture in humanity's earthly voyage, although my own experience has pointed in precisely the opposite direction for the source of their culture's genius. While I am utterly unqualified to discount Mayan connections to spirit beings from other realms, my heartfelt sense is that some of their most valuable Mayan guidance for us comes not from distant stars, but from their culture's powerful connections with the physical planet beneath their feet. These eminently practical lessons from the Maya have the potential to "ground" our lives more harmoniously into nature's infinitely complex ways, to widen our perspectives on human existence, and to help us develop our innate capacity for experiencing shared awareness with those around us.

Mayan traditions have emerged from the living Earth like an ancestral *yax te'*, an ancient kapok tree,[3] more than a hundred generations thick. This ceiba, as it's more commonly known, represents the archetypal Mayan World Tree, the horizontal axis of the cosmos with its deep roots drawing life-giving nutrients from the earth and its trunk reaching toward the star-bejeweled heavens above. A multi-millennially enriched cultural sap flows from deep ancestral roots skyward into the tree's divergent ethnic branches. Each bough grows with its own unique shape and puts forth distinctive blossoms of experientially acquired wisdom. Through reproductive metamorphosis these culturally specific patterns enter into more solid embodiments, the maturing fruit that ripen into the current generation of precious Mayan babies. The Maya—like Chinese, Persians, Indians, and other preeminent world cultures—have a multi-millennial written history and a vast wealth of practical knowledge that can inform modern humanity's cultivation of future generations. Their culture, like the others, has dedicated special attention to proper ripening of human fruit. As we approach completion of the thirteenth *pik* cycle in the Mayan Long Count calendar, their ancestral tree is loaded with multicolored buds, poised for a season of particularly abundant cultural flowering, a time when Mayan wisdom can release its sweet fragrance into the intercontinental winds for all humanity to savor.

Mayan wisdom is, of course, in many ways similar to the vast heritage of practical knowledge acquired by ancient peoples worldwide, but what make Maya stand apart from these other global cultural expressions are their relatively large population and their proximity to the United States. Maya make up what is overwhelmingly the largest native cultural nexus in the entire North American continent. In fact, in the entire New World, only the Kechwa[4] of the South American Andes have a comparably large population. This massive Mayan numerical presence has led them into especially intense and sometimes extremely violent confrontations with the dominating tendencies of some in the region's nonindigenous population. The proximity of the Mayan homelands to the United States and the temporary immigration of tens of thousands of Maya into the U.S. working underclass have recently brought this ancient, *truly* American, culture into extensive contact with our modern ways. Maya sometimes suffer as a result of this closeness to the United States, so out of concern for their well-being, it behooves us to be more aware of their traditions. At the same time, a deeper understanding of Mayan culture can be vitally helpful to us as well as we stand paused at this major crossroad, pondering the road ahead on humanity's collective journey. The well-worn cultural paths of the Maya provide potential alternative directions for us. At a moment when many of our own cultural guides seem to have led us astray, the paths first trod by the leathery bare feet of the ancient Maya offer proven options still viable after millennia of use.

I confess that when I first began to hear about the 2012 date, I couldn't help but marvel at some of the outrageous claims and outlandish speculation coming from a few of my fellow New Age spiritual seekers. The recent feature film *2012* added yet another level of fear to this confusing conjecture. In spite of this, as I've delved deeper into the subject and learned from wiser souls, I now find myself far less inclined to dismiss the 2012 phenomenon as I once did, as entirely baseless assertions fed by media and commercial hype.

For example, even though I have had a profound appreciation of Mayan culture for several decades, I was still taken aback when I recently learned that ancient Mayan astronomers were so brilliant that they apparently had the capability to set up their 13 Pik cycle of 1,872,000 days deliberately with a "zero" date on a solar zenith passage (at their latitude) in 3114 BCE and project more than five thousand years forward to a cycle closing date on a winter solstice. This is an astounding intellectual achievement for a preindustrial culture and strong evidence that the Long Count may have been established with astonishing forethought toward the December 21, 2012 date.

Further strengthening the case for the date's potential significance is that Maya have, indeed, described human evolution in terms of advancement through sequential world ages, a concept advocated by almost all of those writing about 2012. According to Mayan mythology, each age's stage of humanity was mercilessly terminated by divinely inspired catastrophes before a more evolved and properly respectful human being could be created. Since several ancient Mayan hieroglyphic texts associate the beginning of the 13 Pik cycle in the Long Count that occurred in 3114 BCE with an era of cosmic creation, wouldn't one possibility be that the end of this massive cycle of time could also imply the end of the current Mayan age and its mythically anticipated destruction? In Mayan lore, the creator beings' previous experiments in fashioning proper human beings failed due to people's lack of capacity for appropriate reverence and genuine appreciation for divine processes. These less-evolved beings were vanquished by the gods in preparation for a subsequent creation that would produce more refined souls. If we look at the world with eyes wide open, we six billion humans are currently witnessing our own period of cataclysmic environmental destruction, circumstances brought about by our collective lack of respect for nature's infinitely complex ways. The similarity between this tragic situation and the mythological destruction of prior human generations in Mayan lore is at least suggestive, if not compelling.

So when people ask "What will happen in 2012?" I now refrain from simplistic answers and try instead to dialogue with them hoping to learn something myself from my questioners. In spite of my uncertainties, there are a few aspects of 2012 thinking that I *do* feel fairly sure about. I feel confident saying that the ancient Maya would have considered the 13 Pik date in 2012 to be an important calendric event. Even if ancient Maya thought of the complete Long Count *pik* cycle as consisting of twenty 144,000-day units rather than thirteen, as some researchers and hieroglyphic texts suggest, given Mayan culture's prioritization of the number thirteen, they undoubtedly would have also seen the fruition of thirteen *pik*s as significant, a fact demonstrated irrefutably by ancient glyphs that will be discussed later. We know Mayan cosmology describes several sequential eras defined by periods of cataclysmic destruction followed by new creation. Since the beginning of the Long Count is explicitly tied to creation events in ancient Mayan iconography and writing, I remain open to the possibility that the close of the 13 Pik cycle could mark the most recent of those "change in era" periods in Mayan myth.

Furthermore, just as our own libraries of vast knowledge and experience would be largely incomprehensible to the ancient Maya, I am equally sure that they were also aware of dimensions of the human experience that we moderns no longer can even imagine. Human consciousness is shaped by our activities and how we focus our attention, and each human culture and every individual does so uniquely. Until relatively recently in our species' history, our brains and our awareness have developed in intimate relationship with the natural world, experience that activates our animal awareness. I use the term "animal" in a most positive sense implying the development of sensory capacities, physical capacities, instinctual skills that develop through generations of direct and deliberate exposure to nature's ways. Even in recent times, I have personally met Maya living barefoot in remote mountainous areas whose awareness, in particular their perception of themselves as integral to nature and in terms of interpersonal empathy, hints at states of consciousness that are almost nonexistent in the "developed" world. Our modern lifestyle largely cuts us off physically from nature, and our being develops within parameters shaped by our logo-centric worldview, severe social fragmentation, and atrophied psychological capacities. How much can we really know with certainty about the cosmos from within these narrow limits of our experientially shaped and culturally specific mental parameters? Might there actually be some sort of entities who are taking this opportunity to facilitate a collective enhancement of human awareness? After all, in my personal experience, overwhelmingly the most impactful influences in my life have been the saintly beings who appeared in unsolicited and unexpected dreams that I'm sure total less than a minute in which I received instantaneous infusions of positively transformative energy that has shaped my core. Couldn't such beings attempt to reach humanity collectively with their influences as well? Who among us can even begin to understand the unseen macro-cycles that integrate the fathomless universe? Our current best "scientific" guess is that we are hurling at incalculable speeds through incomprehensively vast, infinite space with but barely a clue as to who we are or where we are going. In this limitless all-directional cosmic context, we humans are ill-prepared for saying much definitive about very much at all, much less about such extraordinarily esoteric concepts as world ages and the evolution of consciousness.

Instead of solid answers, I find that more questions arise. Might the recent "return" of the Long Count calendar into human awareness, after an absence of many centuries, be an archetypal alarm clock

ringing in from Jung's collective unconscious? Might personal mythologies about the Maya and 2012 developed by New Age mystics
take on a life of their own and coalesce into real change on a societal
scale through processes of self-fulfilling prophecy? Is 2012 merely an
ingenious New Age marketing scheme or is it a subtle tipping point in
humanity's collective consciousness toward heightened spiritual illumination? Might it be both? I simply don't know.

I sincerely doubt there will be any peak moment of terrestrial catastrophe in connection with the passing of 13 Pik. I certainly hope there
won't be. My best guess is that our earthen orb will make its daily spin
on its axis just as on any other Friday on early-twenty-first-century
planet Earth, with all its everyday horrific and awe-inspiring share of
natural disasters, warfare, environmental degradation, personal and
societal breakthroughs and breakdowns. For those not looking for
any deeper meaning, the day will likely come and go as an "indig-
enously" flavored version of the Y2K nonevent with its survivalist
excitement over potential millennial computer glitches. Yet even as
I remind myself of our vast cosmic framework and urge you to rest
easy concerning disaster scenarios linked to 2012, I still feel com-
pelled to sound an alarm calling more attention to the all-too-real
global catastrophes of ecological and societal disintegration that are
occurring as I write these words. As we enter the era of 2012 we find
ourselves increasingly disconnected from nature's patterns, ever more
insensitive to our collective assault on complex and fragile ecosystems about which we humans have but a glimmer of understanding.
Species are disappearing at rates unknown since the mass extinction
event that killed off the dinosaurs more than sixty million years ago.
One hundred million tons of plastic trash currently spin in the North
Pacific Gyre and through photo-degradation eventually pass into the
tissues of marine wildlife in molecular-sized particles. There is now
no place on our planet untouched by the chemical by-products of
our disintegrated lifestyles. Such contaminants now produce some
40 percent of human deaths worldwide.[5] We seem equally oblivious
to the generalized abuse of our own bodies, "supersizing" ourselves

into unprecedented extremes of physical and psychological degeneration. In the United States we have, on average, more than one hundred foreign chemicals stored in our bodies[6] and increasingly we add to the mix by placing our children on psychiatric drugs in an act of mercy to help them cope with the incoherency and superficiality of the world we've created for them. Human-made hormone-mimicking contaminants currently produce sexual mutations in a growing number of species, from bass to alligators; and we now are finding that they adversely affect the human fetus as well. These are only a few salient examples of a planetary crisis in which humanity is only capable of perceiving the most obvious dimensions of the destruction it has caused.

Regardless of what one thinks about 2012 and the Mayan calendar, if we do not change humanity's direction, the unprecedented human -induced environmental changes on our planet will become even more catastrophic. There is no question that humanity has reached a crossroads. The natural world bestowed upon us by infinitely complex processes of creation, in many very real ways, *is* actually ending. The coincidence between this ubiquitous environmental ruin and the world age philosophy embedded in both Mayan myth and 2012 ideology is irresistibly suggestive. As mentioned earlier, each Mayan world age comes to fruition with apocalyptic disaster in order to create more evolved forms. The earliest attempts at creation yielded the animals of the planet. Next, a human being was made from mud but quickly dissolved. Then came people made from wood who were eventually destroyed by floods and who even had their own tools, their own technology, turn against them (sound familiar?). The current age's human beings were fashioned by the Mayan creator beings from corn[7] ground by the mythical divine Mother herself. Might it now be time for the creators to fashion even more refined beings than we people of corn, ones more capable of living in better harmony with the varied and complex ecosystems of our planet and ones more appreciative of our role in this infinitely vast cosmos? Might the Maya's experientially informed appreciation of nature offer us direction?

Mayan journalist Patricio Balona says:

> For thousands of years and in contemporary Mayan com-
> munities, caring for nature that gives us our resources has
> been a part of our lives. And that care comes with the study
> of the stars, the winds, rain and the changes that each yearly
> cycle's end brings. These factors guide the manner in which
> we care for everything in our environment. We are aware
> that if we unconscientiously exploit what the Creator has
> given us, we surely are headed toward an end.

Could the world as humans have known it be shifting toward some
sort of end? Might it already be too late? Is there some way we can
become more whole and less exploitive? As we witness nature's fabric torn, societal bonds undone, and individual human threads come
loose, I am inspired by the connective orientation of Mayan weavers
I've known as they patiently kneel on their earthen patios, nimbly tie
together broken threads on their backstrap looms, and then reintegrate
the astutely repaired strands back into the larger fabric. The Mayan
cultural paradigm tends toward keeping things whole—be it a community, the natural world, or the cloth of a woman's intricately brocaded
blouse. Traditional Maya have a remarkably sturdy cultural fabric that
has endured and recovered from environmental cataclysm and periods
of societal disintegration. It is woven with practical sensibilities learned
from thousands of years of deliberately intensive interactions with
the tropical ecosystems of their Middle American homelands. As with
many indigenous peoples around the world, Mayan intimacy with the
realm of plants, animals, and other life that sustains them can lead to a
profound awareness of their integrity with what they sometimes refer
to as their "Mother," nature herself. They truly "get" that we humans
are, at least from one very real perspective, simply another animal.
We all suckle in Mother Earth's mountainous arms, wrapped in the
"fabric" of her forests, nourishing ourselves with her life-giving waters.

The genuine sense of familiarity that some traditional Maya have
with the Earth occurs simultaneously with a broadly shared capacity

for compassion fostered through deliberate nurturing of their infants, ingenious childrearing practices based on modeling of parental behavior, and the intentional cultivation of community awareness. As a consequence of these time-proven patterns of behavior, many Maya, at least those not already caught up in our globalized commercial "culture," still experience potent psychological bonds with one another almost impossible for those of us caught up in the distractions of our commercially oriented external environment to imagine. In many cases they also share an experiential awareness of their oneness with the natural world around them. The hard-earned lessons that produce these more integrated states of consciousness are Mayan culture's sacred offering to humanity even though, given the Mayan love of humility, I doubt many of them would ever make such a claim.

As 13 Pik and the much-heralded year 2012 approach, Mayan pathways potentially provide at least potential directions for beginning to mitigate and heal the severe and sometimes irreparable damage we have done to our home planet and the equally harsh physical and psychological wounds we have inflicted upon our children and ourselves. Their traditions call us to place our feet firmly upon the life-giving earth, to lightheartedly pick up our individual life's *cargo* of burdens and blessings, and then set out in earnest on the ancient trails first laid out by the ancestral *mam*[8] millennia ago and still traveled by millions of Maya in the twenty-first century.

13 Pik: December 21, 2012

No one really knows, of course, if any extraordinary events will occur in the portentous year 2012, but human curiosity combined with easy access to electronic communication have led to a lively and multidimensional worldwide social movement surrounding the date, the so-called "2012 phenomenon."[9] Just as in the period leading up to Y2K, there is already an astonishing volume of attention to the 2012 date on the internet in dozens of languages. Simultaneously, a rapidly growing number of books, videos, workshops, and internet communities speculate wildly as to the underlying meaning of the 2012 date and what transformative events might take place. Since José Argüelles first brought my attention to the 2012 date in 1987 with publication of *The Mayan Factor: Path Beyond Technology,* the 2012 phenomenon has expanded exponentially, in spite of the fact that few of us have had the chance to understand its content with critical awareness and with adequate appreciation for Mayan ways.

The ancient Maya, of course, did not know of our current Gregorian calendar and so never made reference to our year 2012. Instead they probably called this special day "13 Pik."[10] The term *pik* refers to the current cycle of 144,000 days in the Mayan Long Count, one of three principal calendars used by the ancient Maya during the so-called Classic Period of their culture (roughly 250–900 CE). This calendar, which fell into disuse among the Maya many centuries ago, is similar to our own calendar in that it counts forward from a fixed "zero" date. For the ancient Maya, this "start" date was August 11, 3114 BCE[11] and they associated it consistently with myths concerning cosmic creation. Counting forward from that "zero" date in the Long Count, days, known individually as *k'in,* were grouped into units of twenty called *winik* by the ancients. Eighteen of these twenty-day *winik* units formed a larger unit of 360 days equal to an approximate year known to the ancient Maya as a *haab* and to modern researchers as a *tun.* Twenty of these approximate years formed a still larger unit of 7,200 days called a *k'atun* (the ancient name may have been *winikhaab*). We know from the hieroglyphs that *k'atun* endings were commonly celebrated by the ancient Maya and the numerous *Chilam Balam* texts from the Yucatán show that the importance of the *k'atun* continued, in what Maya called the *may* count, through the entirety of Spanish colonial rule. The ancient Maya combined twenty *k'atun* periods to form the *pik,* a cycle of 144,000 days or approximately 394 solar (365-day) years. Maya counting of *pik* cycles gradually faded, along with use of the Long Count and hieroglyphic writing, after the Classic Period but scattered clandestine usage of these ancient cultural features probably extended into, and even through, the colonial period. The word *baktun* was invented early in the twentieth century by archaeologists who had still not deciphered the ancient writing system and so were unaware of the original word. It is also the term now adopted by many contemporary Maya from the Guatemalan highlands for referring to the 2012 date. We currently are in the final years of the thirteenth *baktun,* or as the ancients said, *oxlahun pik.* The last written Mayan reference to this ancient term may have been in the *Chilam Balam of Chumayel* in the phrase *oxlahun pik tz'ak,*[12] which researchers associate with the beginning of the 13 *baktun* cycle in 3114 BCE rather than its coming cycle closure in 2012, both referred to with the term "thirteen *pik.*"

Given the profound significance of the number thirteen in Mayan culture and the date's explicit appearance in the hieroglyphs on Monument 6 from Tortuguero, Mexico, it appears that the ancient Maya viewed a sequence of thirteen *pik*s as forming a still larger cycle of 1,872,000 days (more than 5,125 solar years) that some investigators refer to as the "Great Cycle." While there is legitimate scholarly debate concerning the exact day that will mark this cycle's end, I find myself siding wholeheartedly with the few Maya I know who are familiar with the 2012 date and who all prefer December 21 because it comes on the day 4 Ahaw in their 260-day Mayan ritual calendar. We have known since the nineteenth century that the Great Cycle began on a day associated by the ancient Maya with cosmic creation on 4 Ahaw. Since this 1,872,000-day cycle is divisible by 260, the passage of thirteen *pik*s must bring us once again to another 4 Ahaw day. The December 21 date is confirmed in the aforementioned Tortuguero text, the one and only reference to the 2012 date in the entirety of ancient Mayan history. This seventh-century stone monument states unambiguously that the "thirteenth *pik* will be finished (on) 4 Ahaw, the third of K'ank'in."[13] The December 21 / 4 Ahaw date also turns out to be the winter solstice in the Northern Hemisphere. I first saw this as an interesting coincidence, since solstices seem to have minimal importance in the ancient Mayan texts. But I then recalled that the 13 Pik cycle's "zero" date more than five thousand years ago occurred on a solar zenith passage at the latitude where the calendar was probably invented, and I find myself unable to set aside such a remarkable mathematical and astronomical accomplishment as mere chance. Scholars have suggested that the *tzolkin* calendar was developed based on the time between solar zeniths in the Mesoamerican tropics, in particular the 260-day gap between the August and May zeniths at latitude 15 degrees north in the area where the Mayan calendars were likely invented. In establishing their Long Count calendar "zero" date on the August 11, 3114 BCE solar zenith passage, the ancients also imbedded their *tzolkin* ritual cycle, which comes full circle 260 days later on the spring solar zenith passage.

It is important to point out that this so-called Great Cycle was only a minor component within far larger periods of time that theoretically extended infinitely backward and forward in time using a system of exponentially increasing temporal cycles without beginning or end. Contrary to what some say about the date, no Mayan calendar "ends" on 13 Pik. The day merely marks the close of a large time cycle. This and the various other Mayan measurements of time are perpetual in nature, just like our own Gregorian calendar.

When examining the rapidly growing and evolving cultural phenomenon surrounding the 13 Pik date, one cannot help admire the consistency of altruistic attitudes among participants. Even those making the most outrageous and baseless claims seem committed to a more sustainable and healthy relationship with our natural environment and to more enlightened ways of being human. While fully appreciating that commitment, it must also be pointed out that little content in the 2012 phenomenon has much substantive basis in the Mayan world. Apart from the recent publication *13 Baktun: Mayan Visions of 2012 and Beyond* by Mayan novelist Gaspar González, nearly all writings on the subject of 2012 have been written by non-Maya who have minimal experiential familiarity with the Mayan world.[14]

Since most of what we hear and read concerning the Maya in the 2012 phenomenon and about the 13 Pik date comes to us from sources outside the Mayan world, if we hope to gain a better-informed appreciation of the year's potential significance we must first look to the

Maya themselves for answers. Ancient hieroglyphic texts and codices, the *Popol Vuh*,[15] the books of the *Chilam Balam*, and the works of contemporary Maya are our best resources. The living voices of today's Maya connect us directly to the human "frequency" of the Mayan world, and their words can inspire new appreciation for their rich heritage. I, of course, cannot speak for the Maya; my sense is that many of them understand me far better than I do their world.

The 2012 Phenomenon

A recent Google search requesting online items that included both the terms "Maya" and "2012" produced more than four million electronic references, a figure that has doubled in less than one year![16] This massive and expanding internet presence mirrors a rapidly growing virtual library of books and other media focusing on the topic. I have attempted to stay abreast of this 2012 phenomenon for several years and now feel familiar with the main ideological currents that circulate there. Given the extraordinary level of public interest in the Mayan calendar and this anxiously anticipated date, it has been surprising to find that most materials currently circulating about 2012 have only superficial connections to the realities of the Mayan world and that the overwhelming majority of the content in the 2012 phenomenon is inadequately researched misinformation.

To some extent, this is because the Maya themselves have thus far had relatively little input into shaping our thinking about 2012. Even today, only a tiny number of Maya have had any exposure to the topic.[17] The Long Count calendar that the 2012 date emerges from fell into disuse well before the arrival of the Spanish invaders in the sixteenth century, and knowledge of its rediscovery by Western academics has reached extremely few of today's Maya apart from the most educated. In fact, if you could somehow randomly select a hundred adults from across the Mayan world, I think you would be fortunate to find even a single person who has even heard of 2012, much less a Maya who could tell you something about its significance. Ironically, given its supposedly Mayan underpinnings, the 2012 phenomenon has been almost exclusively non-Maya; but as 2012 makes its way into popular media in the Mayan area, as it is certain to do, these circumstances will change quickly and may have strong social and political impacts, especially in Guatemala.

Contrary to what many of my colleagues in the academic community assume, the 2012 phenomenon's origins are not in New Age circles but lie instead within the ivory tower itself. The first contemporary reference to the potential significance of the date was made by an astronomer at Vassar College named Maud Makemson, who stated in 1951 that "the completion of a great cycle of thirteen *baktuns* would indeed be an occasion of the highest expectation" for the Maya.[18] Some fifteen years later, the esteemed Mayanist Michael Coe mentioned that "there is a suggestion ... that Armageddon would overtake the degenerate peoples of the world and all creation on the final day of the thirteenth *[baktun]*. Thus ... our present universe [would] be annihilated ... when the Great Cycle of the Long Count reaches completion." Since then, due to the extraordinary volume of unfounded speculation that has arisen in the last two decades surrounding 2012, this cultural phenomenon has fallen into extreme disrepute among most serious scholars. In fact, academic disdain for the hyperbole of the 2012 phenomenon has reached such an intense level that the primary computer Listserv for Mayan scholars, Aztlan-L, now explicitly bans all 2012-related posts, and the esteemed archaeoastronomer Anthony Aveni has dedicated an entire book to discounting what he views as 2012 madness, labeling it "the fashion of our times."[19]

While interest in 2012 first surfaced in the scholarly community, New Age thinkers are overwhelmingly responsible for bringing this extraordinary date into the public imagination. In 1975 three different references to the date were published. The great novelist of the Southwestern United States, Frank Waters, discussed the coming Long Count cycle closing in his book *Mexico Mystique: The Coming Sixth World of Consciousness* and explored its connections with Hopi prophetic traditions. That same year, Terence McKenna wrote about 2012 in *The*

Invisible Landscape: Mind, Hallucinogens, and the I Ching, arriving at the date through his substance-enhanced insights into the nature of time and its relationship to what he saw in human history as an exponential increase in the rate of novelty. That same year, Mexican-American visionary artist and spiritual teacher José Argüelles mentioned 2012 in *The Transformative Vision: Reflections on the Nature and History of Human Expression.*

In 1987, Dr. Argüelles established himself as the virtual "father" of the 2012 phenomenon with publication of *The Mayan Factor: Path Beyond Technology,* an enigmatic work that inspired thousands, including me, to entertain his bold and unique perspectives on the Maya and their calendars. Argüelles is also responsible for what he called the Harmonic Convergence that took place in August 1987, an event that I recall participating in with my young family by taking part in our invented version of a sweat lodge "ceremony" in the company of dear friends on a dairy farm in upstate New York. Argüelles states that this worldwide event marked "the exponential acceleration of the wave harmonic of history as it phases into a moment of unprecedented synchronization,"[20] words that are suggestive of the often cryptic (for me at least) nature of his work. The jacket of his best-known book, *The Mayan Factor,* called the 1987 date a "shift point into the last 25 years of the galactic beam," a beam presumably due to shift once again in 2012, ushering in a period of radically enhanced human consciousness. In the text, Argüelles revealed that before writing the book, he had "come to feel the spiritual presence of the Maya,"[21] words that assured readers like me that his beliefs arose from the inner realms of the indigenous soul.

In 1993, he revealed that he had come into contact with what he called Telektonon, the "Talking Stone of Prophecy."[22] Telektonon purportedly revealed itself to Argüelles in a channeled message delivered through the stone "tube" that extends upstairs from the crypt of the famed seventh-century Mayan king K'inich Hanaab' Pakal, in the Temple of the Inscriptions in Palenque, Mexico. (This curious archaeological feature actually exists.) Since then, Argüelles has acted as spokesperson for this ancient Mayan lord, proposing a global shift to a thirteen-month lunar calendar that he invented with the hope that it would bring humanity into closer alignment with celestial rhythms.

While Argüelles approaches many aspects of Mayan culture with engaging creativity, one of his boldest inventions has been development of his personal version of the 260-day Mayan ritual calendar, a system that he nestles within a solar calendar consisting of thirteen months of twenty-eight days plus an additional "day out of time." Argüelles openly acknowledges the fundamental discrepancies between his own 260-day calendar called Dreamspell and that used by contemporary Maya in the Guatemalan highlands. He explains that his own calendar is "Galactic Maya" rather than "Indigenous Maya"[23] and that his combination of twenty "solar seals" and thirteen "galactic tones" has its own validity apart from any resemblance it bears to the Mayan *cholq'ih*, more commonly known as the *tzolkin*, the 260-day ritual calendar. His gracious demeanor and extensive work with New Age audiences around the planet have created a situation in which his invented "Mayan" calendar may be even more widely known outside of the Mayan world than the actual ritual calendar that Mayan daykeepers have patiently developed and maintained in a continuous tradition dating back well more than two thousand years. Argüelles refers to his work and followers as "New Dispensation Maya,"[24] and he has taken the name Valum Votan ("Closer of the Cycle") for use in his work spreading what he says are prophecies from the seventh-century Bakal Ahaw (Lord of Bone). His vision for 2012 is bold and idealistic, holding that "We are leaving the old time of war and conflict, where time is money, and entering a new time of peace and harmony, where *time is art*."[25] He posits that "a resonant frequency phase shift will usher us into the brilliance of galactic-solar-planetary evolution. We shall pass not only into a post-historic, but a post-human, or super human phase of our evolution."[26] My sincerest wish is that Dr. Argüelles' profoundly optimistic visions of humanity's future prove true.

A relative newcomer to the 2012 phenomenon, biologist Carl Johan Calleman, has already made an impressive impact on the 2012 phenomenon with several books on the topic, beginning with the 2000 publication of *Solving the Greatest Mystery of Our Time: The Mayan Calendar*. In many ways, he follows in the footsteps of Argüelles by arguing that the Mayan Long Count functions as a temporal expression that reflects an exponentially increasing rate in the evolution of human consciousness, a process that he believes will culminate in conjunction with fruition of the current Long Count *pik* cycle. Argüelles, noting the strong similarities in their approaches to Mayan material, wrote the foreword for Dr. Calleman's highly popular 2004 book, *The Mayan Calendar and the Transformation of Consciousness*. Like Argüelles, Calleman envisions a global spiritual awakening that the ancient Maya foresaw millennia ago. According to Dr. Calleman's calculations, however, the cycle ending, at least in terms of its spiritual dimensions, will occur on October 28, 2011, rather than in December 2012. His choice of this alternate date appears to be based on the fact that October 28, 2011, falls on the day 13 Ahaw on the *cholq'ih*, arguably the most auspicious day in the ritual calendar.

Several other keenly insightful, talented, and provocative writers, such as Daniel Pinchbeck and Gregg Braden, have added their unique perspectives to 2012 lore, but no one stands out in terms of his research on the Maya and his influence on the 2012 phenomenon more than independent researcher John Major Jenkins. Unfortunately, some serious scholars have tended to confuse his work with the extremes of misinformation common elsewhere in 2012 literature or get sidetracked by Jenkins' speculation concerning the date's metaphysical implications, a realm deliberately avoided in most academic circles, but one I feel Jenkins should be free to explore. In the process of reevaluating my own thinking on 2012, especially on the basis of my own numerous conversations with contemporary Maya in Mexico and Guatemala, I have found that I cannot resist speculating on the date myself and now find myself embracing John Jenkins' willingness to investigate potential explanations for the date's significance. If academia can dispassionately look at the heart of his thesis, setting aside what others in the 2012 phenomenon have said and granting this independent researcher the option to wonder about our collective future, our understanding of the Mayan world may be enriched by Jenkins' perspectives.

Jenkins calls our attention to the potential astronomical and astrological significance of the date, asserting that the Maya established the Long Count cognizant not only of the solar zenith passage on 4 Ahaw in 3114 BCE that began our current era, but also with an eye to the astronomy at the time of the 13 Pik cycle closing on the Northern Hemisphere winter solstice in 2012. In his 1998 book, *Maya Cosmogenesis 2012,* easily one of the best researched of the popular books that focus on the 2012 date, he contends that Classic Mayan astronomers set the Long Count on the 2012 solstice date after noting an extremely rare[27] alignment on that day between Earth, the sun, and the dark rift in the Milky Way galaxy.[28]

In his own words:

> Since the early 1990s, my work has been oriented toward reconstructing the authentic Mayan beliefs about 2012. My attention to the likelihood that December 21, 2012, was an intentional artifact of the creators of the Long Count was derived by the fact that according to most widely agreed-upon correlation, the cycle ending falls on a solstice. I took the common-sense approach of examining the site, Izapa, belonging to the Izapan culture, that many scholars felt was responsible for the formulation of the Long Count calendar during the pre–Classic Period. My findings indicated a rare astronomical alignment, referred to generally as "the galactic alignment" but more precisely as "the alignment of the December solstice sun with the dark rift in the Milky Way." In *Maya Cosmogenesis 2012* I showed how the dark rift and other features involved in this alignment were utilized by the Maya in their ball game symbolism, the creation mythology, king-making rites, and were encoded into the iconography and archaeoastronomical alignments at Izapa. This

work has been largely ignored or misrepresented by critics. Today, Tortuguero Monument 6 is receiving a great deal of attention because it contains a Classic Period inscription (ca. 669 AD) and a date reference to December 21, 2012. A thorough analysis of the thirteen dates on the monument, undertaken by Michael Grofe and myself, reveals that four of the thirteen dates involve alignments of the sun with the dark rift (the one in 2012 is on the solstice, which relates it to a unique era of precessional alignment). Two other dates involve alignment of the dark rift with Jupiter (at station) and a lunar eclipse.[29]

Jenkins is a humble and serious researcher who exhibits solid understanding of Mayan calendar systems and the related astronomy. His core thesis depends on whether or not Mayan astronomers knew of the long-term celestial shifts resulting from precession, an effect produced by the Earth's wobble that manifests in an apparent slow shift in the constellations of the night sky that is detectable only after hundreds of years of observation. Since the ancient Maya could keep accurate records across generations using their hieroglyphic and numerical systems, and were highly attentive to apparent celestial dynamics, such a supposition seems quite plausible, I would even say likely. We need to recall the extreme astronomical and mathematical sophistication that was required for the ancient Maya to set up this major calendric cycle of 1,872,000 days with a beginning on a solar zenith passage and an end point on a winter solstice. This Long Count cycle began with the sun directly overhead and on a day that started a 260-day count until the next zenith passage in May. It will end on the winter solstice, the shortest day of the year. The truly impressive skills required for accomplishing this task would seem to make the discovery of precession a relatively simple matter of detailed record-keeping.

According to Jenkins, ancient Mesoamerican astronomer/astrologers established the Long Count to signal what he terms the "galactic alignment" of the 2012 winter solstice sun with the dark rift of the

Milky Way. Like Argüelles and Calleman, he believes that the close of the 13 Pik cycle heralds a shift in eras and potentially to a new age of greatly enhanced human awareness. Jenkins sees the Mexican site of Izapa as the birthplace of this "galactic alignment" philosophy and specifically points to the iconography near the Group F ballcourt and its alignment to the winter solstice as evidence in support of his ideas. When I first came upon Jenkins's work, like my other colleagues in academia, I was confused by his speculation as to the cosmic and societal implications of the date. But I have now learned more about Mayan astronomy and find myself easily able to set aside his "galactic" speculation as being beyond my own limitations of understanding. As a consequence, I now believe that Jenkins is right, at least about the ancients considering the culmination of the thirteenth *pik* cycle to have been significant and also that they knowingly established their Long Count calendar with a set point on the Northern Hemisphere winter solstice that occurs at the time of the cycle closing. Not only does the Tortuguero text referred to previously in this chapter explicitly mention the 4 Ahaw, 13 Pik date on December 21, 2012, but Dr. Aveni has shown that precisely in the area where the calendar likely originated there was a strong tendency to orient construction in alignment with solstices at the ancient sites. Furthermore, he says the entire site of Izapa, not just the ballcourt referred to by Jenkins, is oriented toward the solstices.[30] Jenkins's new evidence derived from the Tortuguero text that shows ancient Mayan interest in the intersect between heavenly bodies on the ecliptic arc and the dark rift could prove significant in strengthening acceptance of his "galactic alignment" theory. Although I do not think there is yet enough unambiguous evidence to conclude that Mayan astronomers were also targeting Jenkins's "galactic alignment" between the Earth, sun, and Milky Way with their Long Count, the likelihood that they were tracking precessional shifts combined with their mathematical expertise lead me to value his theory as an invaluable perspective worth considering as our understanding of Mayan hieroglyphics and iconography improves and as there are new findings from the archaeological digs.

Mayan Teachers

The 2012 phenomenon boasts luminaries like Argüelles, Jenkins, Calleman, Pinchbeck, Braden, and others; but there are also several New Age figures who are of Mayan ancestry, and one assumes that living indigenous traditions substantively inform these Mayan teachers' thinking on the 2012 subject and lend a greater sense of cultural authenticity to 2012 ideology. Undoubtedly, the best known of the genuinely Mayan teachers among New Age spiritual practitioners has been Hunbatz Men, a Mayan spiritual guide and cultural activist from the "Itza lineage." At its core, Men's is a compassionate message warmly presented with poetic awareness of language. He was privileged to enjoy a small Mayan community upbringing under the spiritual tutelage of his uncle, Don Beto. His public work as a Mayan spiritual teacher really began in earnest in the 1980s, when Men was already in his forties. His inspirational creativity and his multifaceted life have enriched him with a diverse range of influences. He studied Gnostic philosophy and fine arts in Mexico City, worked as a commercial artist in New York City, and currently serves as a much-sought-after spiritual guide and ceremonial leader at the Cosmic International Mayan Community Lol Be near Mérida, the bustling capital city of the Mexican state of Yucatán. Men has been particularly active in opening up Mayan archaeological sites for conducting rituals, and he leads group tours of spiritual seekers to reconsecrate those sites as initiation centers in preparation for a coming "Itza era." He recently organized a group tour in the Mayan world in order to donate an oracle crystal skull to the sons of the late Mayan elder Chan K'in Viejo as representatives of the Lacandon Maya. The crystal skulls are a phenomenon unto themselves, thirteen quartz skulls known for their capacity to transmit information with "cosmic rays." According to Men, the Maya have lived in several other parts of the world since ancient times, including Egypt, India, and even Atlantis.[31] Men's teachings and spiritual work have provided genuine inspiration for many spiritual seekers even though some of his beliefs concerning worldwide

Mayan influences and Atlantean origins do not appear clearly in the archaeological record nor are they ideas shared by Maya in general. Men's genuinely warm demeanor, transparently positive intentions, and the fact that he actually *is* Maya have attracted many sincere and dedicated students.

Revered K'iche' Mayan elder Alejandro Cirilo Pérez Oxlaj stands out as one of the most traditional of the few Mayan teachers connected with the 2012 phenomenon. *Tat* Cirilo,[32] affectionately known as *tata* (father), was born in Quetzaltenango, the second largest city of Guatemala, and raised in the nearby village of San Francisco El Alto. According to his wife, he received his sacred *vara*, the bundle of holy *tz'ite (Erythrina corallodendron)* seeds cherished by highland Mayan oracles, at the age of thirteen from his father. Upon doing so, he established the thirteenth generation of Mayan spiritual guides in his family. Later in life, in a revelatory experience, "invisible beings" gave him the name Wakatel Utiw (Wandering Wolf) and a mandate as "the Voice of the Jungle" and a "messenger of the Maya."[33] From his current home in Antigua Guatemala, he heads the Consejo Nacional de Ancianos Mayas de Guatemala, one of the largest of several multiethnic associations of Mayan elders. He also serves in the government of President Álvaro Colom as Guatemala's official international ambassador for its indigenous peoples from an office in the National Palace. As part of his mission, he travels the world as a representative of the Maya, sharing prophecies and a message of compassion, fearlessness, and respect in preparation for the coming period of world transition. The core of his message comes from his own K'iche' oral tradition. He says his own elders repeated the following message from their ancestors: "In the time of 12 *baktun* and 13 *Ahaw* is the return of the ancient ones, the return of the men of wisdom. May the morning come, may the dawn come, so the people can have peace and be happy."[34] Keeping true to these words, *tat* Cirilo repeatedly urges people not to be afraid about 2012, and to instead look forward to a period of positive transformation.

Mayan Oral Prophecies of World Changes

Just as *tat* Cirilo's words above demonstrate, even though much in the 2012 phenomenon has little basis in the Mayan world, there are very real prophetic currents that exist within many contemporary Mayan communities that refer to world change. Like those in the New Age 2012 movement, these indigenous beliefs point to an approaching period of significant, even catastrophic, world change, but they typically do not specify the year 2012. For example, within the prophetic tradition of the Macewal[35] Maya in the Yucatán Peninsula, there has long existed a belief in a rapidly approaching cataclysmic period of warfare that will lead to the destruction of the current world and the creation of a new Mayan society. According to Paul Sullivan, Maya of one Macewal village believed in 1989 that war was "not much further off than the year 2000 and that it is inevitable."[36] According to one Mexican anthropologist, "the wait for fulfillment of the promises of the Cross, the imminent arrival of the end of the world and the creation of a new Mayan society are dynamic elements that are present, strong, alive, and active."[37] It bears mentioning that the temporal focus of this world-ending war around the year 2000 may have arisen from recent Christian millenarian currents since Nelson Reed's lengthy study of the Macewal noted no such specificity during his visit to the region in 1959.[38]

In recent years I have made several trips to the Macewal area specifically to speak with those familiar with their prophetic traditions and I have had the rare opportunity to make offerings at all of their principal shrines under the supervision of the temple guardians. In every case, those involved confirmed that there is a generalized expectation of major upheaval and world change among those most closely associated with the shrine sites. At one site, the main prayer-maker for the little chapel said that the only reason that divinely inspired annihilation of humanity has not yet occurred is a result of God's mercy for our innocent babies. We adults are guilty of violating sacred ways, especially in regard to our environmental misbehavior. A

Yukatek-speaking friend who was translating for me summarized the prayer-maker's thinking on the difficult times ahead:

> When the end comes, the world will be overwhelmed by huge balls of fire descending from the sky, cutting swaths through humanity. But it will not destroy all humans. Some will survive. It is then that the Creator will send a monster to catch the stragglers, who by then will be making their way to sanctuary at the Macewal ceremonial centers. But even if you don't get eaten by the monster, you will have to be held accountable for all your transgressions on Earth before being allowed into the sanctuary. The Creator will ask you what it is that you have done to remedy your earthly faults and if you do not have a good enough answer, you will be whipped and then allowed into the shrine site.[39]

In an extraordinary demonstration of generosity, the prayer-maker guarding this particular shrine invited my Mayan friend and I to return there with our families when it becomes clear that this inevitable destruction is at hand.

The Lacandon Maya, or Hach Winik as they call themselves, are closely related to the Macewal in terms of language. Among the few remaining Lacandon Mayan traditionalists still living in Chiapas, Mexico, there has also been a belief that the end of the world is at hand. In 1978, the late well-known spiritual leader Chan K'in had stated, "Our Lord Hach Akyum will make everything die.... The grass wishes to die. The seed, the animals all wish to die. And the True People [the Lacandon] also—we all die. In thirty years Hach Akyum will destroy the world."[40]

The end-of-the-world tradition is so strong among the Hach Winik (Lacandon) that they have a special word for it, *xu'tan*. Even though at this point nearly all of the Hach Winik in all three of their principal settlements have converted to Christian denominations, as I found on two visits there, recognition of the term *xu'tan* persists. Several

Lacandon men recently made clear to me that the Christian apocalypse they have learned about in their local churches and the Mayan
xu'tan are not the same thing. For them, *xu'tan* particularly implies the
cutting, burning, and destruction of vegetation. As in the case of the
Macewal Mayan beliefs concerning world renewal, those of the Lacandon reflect their own peculiar historical circumstances as witnesses to
the virtual elimination of their traditional homeland, the Selva Lacan-
dona, once one of the largest rainforests in our continent. The living
green world that nurtured Lacandon culture for hundreds of years is
now almost completely gone. Having witnessed this ongoing deforestation, the Lacandon beliefs in impending world destruction seem
quite logical. Coincidentally, they also parallel the cataclysmic dimensions in the 2012 movement.

My recent visits to two of the three principal Lacandon settlements
confirm that many of these beliefs are persistent even with the om-
nipresence there of evangelical Christianity. One man told of a prophetic dream he had recently concerning humans' lack of respect for
nature and the destruction of the forest cover. He dreamed that as
he was headed to his *milpa* (corn garden) he heard loud stomping.
He cautiously approached the direction of the sound and saw trees—
some sick ones, some dried ones, and some healthy ones—walking
to a clearing in the woods. As he got closer he heard them talking
about what was ailing them. There was deforestation, carelessly set
fires, and humans' needless cutting of trees. The trees met urgently to
discuss the end they foresaw if humans did not stop their abuse of the
land. The following day after the dream the man went into the forest and heard whispers around him. He sat to contemplate the voices
and after recalling his dream, he understood that the trees were giving him a message—to spread the word that if we don't take care of
our resources, our future generations will not have what our elders
had, the natural world we are watching die day after day. The Lacandon man had never heard of the predictions surrounding 2012 but
seemed convinced that humanity's shortsighted behavior could have
catastrophic consequences.[41]

Recently, knowledge of the year 2012 itself has spread beyond the realm of a select group of internationally known Mayan spiritual teachers and intellectuals to include several spiritual guides still living and working at home within their highland Guatemalan communities. Once Mayan spiritual guides hear about the date, their natural inclination seems to be to incorporate it reflexively with their own prophetic oral traditions. They also tend to envision 2012 with hope for a revival of Mayan cultural practices and indigenous political power. The date's origin in the hieroglyphic writings of their revered ancestors lends immediate credibility to its significance, even though Maya seem far less inclined than non-Maya to reach conclusions as to what exactly the ancients meant to express. Out of modesty and respect, Maya tend not to attempt personal interpretations of messages from those they consider far wiser than themselves.

The K'iche' spiritual guide Rigoberto Itzep[42] recalls listening as a boy of eight or nine to community elders in his remote highland town, saying that their own elders had told them, "You will still see many warnings. You will still see and hear strange things. You will still see great ruin. There will be many changes on Earth." According to Itzep, his K'iche' elders never specified the year 2012, but for him, the potential for the year is multifaceted. For example, Itzep says, "The ideological power of the West in its entirety might expire forever in 2012," words that undoubtedly represent the heartfelt wish of many Maya in the region. While *tat* Rigoberto makes clear that the year 2012 itself did not arise from his K'iche' Mayan oral tradition, he says that the prophecies of ruin and changes that he heard from his elders may indeed be authentic cultural content that he says might be "woven together" with the 13 Pik date in the Long Count.

The fact that we are currently coming to the close of 13 Pik is especially suggestive since the number thirteen expresses maximum potential in the *cholq'ih* calendar and also implies a culmination period that *tat* Rigoberto, a calendar priest, believes could bring about environmental and social upheaval and perhaps a subsequent period of human and ecological renewal. Refusing to say conclusively what will actually happen, he instead prefers to talk about the value in seeing the date as a time for reflection on humanity's behavior. In particular, he expresses concern about our harmful impacts on the natural world. He notes that the 2012 date occurs with the day No'h as year-bearer[43] during a No'h year, using the 365-day *haab* calendar. The No'h year-bearer suggests a period of thoughtfulness. Under the influences of No'h, spirit and body merge in heightened intuition and greater access to the collective memory from the ancestral realm.

But even for Itzep, and other traditional Maya like *tat* Cirilo, the exact date itself in 2012 is not especially critical. Instead, they view the date as simply a temporal marker in the midst of vast cyclical processes that were set in motion long ago. As a young, articulate Mayan spiritual guide from Chichicastenango recently told me: "It is an event that has already begun, there are already signs.... Humans more than ever should pay close attention to all the events that disturb balance. They are teachings that we living beings should extract from the stages through which we pass. It's not that we are arriving at a zero hour in 2012; it's already beginning."[44]

Apart from Maya in Yucatán and lowland Chiapas, a growing number of Mayan cultural activists in Guatemala have expressed similar ideas, but with their recently acquired knowledge of the Long Count, they make explicit reference to 2012. Gaspar González, a Mayan novelist and prominent cultural activist, was certainly among the first Maya to have referred explicitly to the potential import of the year 2012.[45] In 1996, he wondered out loud if the recently ended Guatemalan civil war might have been part of an extended period of severe and horrific tribulation that had helped prepare his people for the next cycle in the human experience. He added that the current age of the human beings made of corn was ending, and that beginning afterward, there will be a societal rebirth into what he called *una nueva era de la luz* (a new age of light). More recently, González added the following comments:

> From the perspective of contemporary Maya, 2012 constitutes a very important point in the history of humanity

since time is a variable that greatly influences the life of the planet and everything that exists on it. Human beings do not exist by coincidence or by a work of chance. They are part of a plan to carry out a mission in this part of the universe. The world is still not totally finished in its creation and perfection; this human creature has a role to play in the world and its preservation. One could say that the life of the planet depends on human beings and what they do in their existence.[46]

As a senior member of the cultural revival movement known as the Movimiento Maya, a serious scholar, a native speaker of Q'anhobal Maya, and a onetime member of the Guatemalan Academy of Mayan Languages, González has impeccable credentials as a Mayan spokesperson. He recently published a book entitled *El 13 Baktun: La nueva era 2012*,[47] which is now available in translation as *13 Baktun: Mayan Visions of 2012 and Beyond*.[48] In this first book written about 2012 to have actually been written by a Maya, he lays out his own and Q'anhobal Mayan beliefs relative to world change. His specific references to the year 2012 undoubtedly are a result of academic study of the once-forgotten Mayan Long Count calendar but they coincide well in terms of content with preexistent prophetic currents such as those among the Hach Winik, Macewal, and highland Maya like *tat* Rigoberto, but these prophetic traditions are not explicit in terms of date.

Another Mayan intellectual, the Jakalteko novelist, professor, and cultural activist Victor Montejo, echoes González's emphasis on the active role of human beings in the coming age after 2012 when he says:

Prophetic expressions of the indigenous peoples insist on the protagonist role that new generations must play at the close of this Oxlanh B'aktun (thirteen B'aktun) and the beginning of the new Maya millennium. The ancestors have always said that "one day our children will speak to the world."… This millennial or b'aktunian movement responds to the close of a great prophetic cycle ... the great prophetic cycle of 400 years in the Maya calendar. For the Maya, this is not the close of the second millennium or two thousand years after Christ, but rather the close of the fifth millennium according to the ancient Mayan calendar initiated in the mythical year that corresponds to 3114 B.C. [correction of typo in original] ... The b'aktun includes the global concept of time and the regeneration of life with new ideas and actions. In other words, the theoretical b'aktunian approach leads us to understand the effect of human ideas and actions on all that exists on the earth and their effects on the environment and cosmos.[49]

Patricio Balona, my friend and the nephew and student of the renowned Mayan healer Don Elijio Pantí, while shying away from directly confirming the specific importance of the 2012 date, echoes the words of Montejo and González by reaffirming that Maya do indeed anticipate change associated with a shift in temporal cycles:

The 2012 speculators, those who do not believe the world will go boom on December 21, 2012, speak of changes, increased consciousness, alignment of heavenly bodies, the end of a cycle. I guess it's just a more sophisticated way of saying what the Maya already know happens at the end of each cycle. It may not be the definition or theory about December 21, 2012 that we are currently hearing, but this knowledge has been as Maya as it can be in Mayan culture.[50]

We may never know with any certainty if the ancient Maya established their Long Count calendar to signal such a shift in 2012. But clearly, the concept of cyclical change into a brighter future with a deliberately more thoughtful humanity is inherent in Mayan thought, apart from the date itself.

Although few living Maya are currently familiar with the year

2012, the concept of a coming world renewal has already captured the imagination of many in the Mayan world through the teachings and preachers of the numerous fundamentalist Christian denominations that have been so successful there.[51] The disastrous earthquake that shook Guatemala in 1976 not only killed more than twenty thousand Mayan villagers, it brought with it a new wave of missionaries hoping to share their fundamentalist religious ideology with the native peoples along with much-needed relief supplies. Maya were drawn to the intensity of the evangelical message and the personal sacrifices required by the new Christians, and the pulpits of the region have been taken over by Mayan ministers speaking in their own languages, a rare ability among Spanish-speaking Catholic priests in the region. The almost apocalyptic violence of the earthquake seemed to set the stage for the particularly brutal military repression of the Mayan population in Guatemala in the late 1970s and early 1980s when thousands of Mayan civilians perished and hundreds of thousands of others found themselves wounded or displaced. While there exist several complementary explanations for the massive Mayan shift toward Christian fundamentalism in recent decades apart from this violent context, when missionaries refer to the coming end of the world in accord with their interpretation of the Bible,[52] one can understand how some Maya might be inclined to believe them. With the earth shaking beneath them, witnessing their families and relatives dying in droves, lamenting a perceived degeneration of their own religious traditions, and seeing a notable decline in the quality of their natural surroundings, it might be a challenge not to conclude otherwise. Fundamentalist groups focus on passages in the biblical book of Revelation and, of course, make no reference to the year 2012. Although there is no evidence that Mayan fundamentalists will embrace the 2012 date, the fact that in specific parts of the Mayan world they literally share the streets and paths of their communities with 2012 adherents makes it virtually unavoidable that the two "apocalyptic" currents will eventually come into contact with one another. Since even evangelical Maya still reflexively hold the elders and ancestors dear, when they hear

about the Mayan origins of the 2012 predictions, it may prove irresistible for them to connect the date with their biblical "end of days"
thinking. Whether or not this explicit connection is made, Maya are
in general agreement that the human journey has reached a critical
juncture.

CHAPTER 2

Finding the Mayan Path

Pilgrims walking through corn to Mayan ceremony in Santiago Atitlán.

My Own Path

My own initial experiences with Mayan culture came as I entered adulthood. The previous several years had been tumultuous; but they came after what, in retrospect, was a remarkably fortunate upbringing. Nearly my entire childhood took place in Kent, a small town with a large university in northeast Ohio. Living near the end of a dead-end street, my friends and I had ready access to our favorite pond, climbing trees with handholds I still remember clearly, a massive boulder left for us during the last ice age by receding glaciers, and a particularly abundant blackberry patch. My father was a geology professor and dean at Kent State University. He planned his research well, taking me along with my mother and two sisters for extended periods of travel abroad to study stream sedimentation, one time camping for two months in gorgeous remote valleys in the eastern Pyrenees of Cataluña.

On another such trip at age thirteen, while in Czechoslovakia for my father to present a paper at an international geological conference, we witnessed the 1968 Soviet invasion put an end to the buds of Prague Spring. I vividly remember all the international visitors who were staying in our hillside campground huddled in the basement of the small restaurant watching tracer bullets streak across the night sky overhead from down below in the city as we listened in silence to the thunderous rumble of the tanks pouring into the city to quell resistance from Czech nationalists. At first, the deafening roar of the MiGs ripping through the sky only hundreds of feet above our heads along with all the other amazing new sights was enthralling for a male teenager. Only when I heard the desperate screams of an old woman whose son had just been shot for taking photographs did my fascination instantly disappear and turn to horror. Less than two years later, the infamous May 4 shootings took place just several hundred yards from my high school in Kent. Armed National Guard troops patrolled our little street, and words like "They should have killed more" in the mouths of local townspeople stung in my ears. Seeing brute violence from both the political left in Prague and from the conservative right in Kent left me politically radicalized in the sense of searching for root causes and solutions rather than adhering to any fixed ideology.

Both my elementary and secondary education took place in the highly enriched environment of the Kent State University School, a tuition-free laboratory school for the training of teachers and educational experimentation, and most of my friends and fellow students were faculty children. As part of this truly extraordinary instruction, we discussed the writings of Malcolm X and international affairs with enthusiastic and politically savvy university graduate students. We listened to the genius of Miles Davis' *Live-Evil* in the school library and joined our teachers in anti–Vietnam War protests along the small street in front of the school. I flourished in this superstimulating environment and was always a straight-A student. Meanwhile, I was repeatedly stunned when childhood heroes were killed by assassins. Nearly every weekday evening, I was riveted to the television screen by the nightly news scenes of battle from Southeast Asia and in America's burning cities.

As I moved on to university studies at Kent State University, our family began to disintegrate. My father and I became deeply estranged, taking radically opposite sides in a rapidly widening generation gap. His experience in Prague had transformed him from a Kennedy Democrat into a speaker for radically conservative student groups such as the Young Americans for Freedom. My attempts to grow out my hair to show my allegiance to counterculture values were a constant source of conflict between us. I was forbidden to see the film *Woodstock* when it came out as he thought it would have a corrupting influence on those who saw it. The air in our house seemed charged with anger and it seemed that it was mostly directed at me.

In the midst of this worsening domestic conflict, my father's life fell apart. Within a two-year period starting when I was in eleventh grade, his extramarital affair was discovered, my parents went through an anguishing divorce, my father remarried, to a woman who treated him poorly, he was diagnosed with pancreatic cancer, and he then died an excruciatingly painful death. In retrospect, his mental anguish and physical suffering seem like punishments he somehow created for himself out of his overwhelming sense of guilt for all the pain he had caused my mother and our family. Some of my clearest memories of these sad times are of driving him to the pointless and nauseating chemotherapy treatments as he sat next to me in sullen despair. In the context of his impending death, the significance of our opposing political ideas and cultural orientations quickly faded into the realm of the meaningless. After he mercifully died on his forty-fifth birthday, it was left to me to greet callers at his funeral. Neither my mother nor his new wife wanted to attend. Life felt raw, fragile, and pointless.

At such a desperate time, my natural inquisitiveness combined with an urgent desire for a more profound life experience led me to use natural "teaching substances" to open the door to deeper insight about the true nature of reality. In doing so, I was afforded innumerable delusion-devastating and humbling insights, liberation from remorse, noticeable permanent and positive transformation, and countless unexpected blessings. Numerous Mesoamerican peoples have used such psyche-illuminating agents in sacred contexts for thousands of years. There are several native groups in Mexico, for example, that still ingest peyote or various psilocybin-bearing mushrooms. Ironically, for those in the United States accustomed to associating any mind-altering agent with social degeneration, the Huichol, Cora, Mazatec, and other peoples who use these substances are also some of the most cohesive, environmentally sustainable, and self-sufficient societies in our continent. When a human consumes these so-called hallucinogens, habitual modes of perception become far more flexible and cohesive ideology sometimes even disappears entirely. By delving below the surface consciousness of the normal patterns of thinking and belief systems, a person reflexively comes to understand these mental constructs as being useful but extremely superficial, and then effortlessly gravitates toward more substantive dimensions of the human experience: our existence as another mammal on the face of the living Earth, our heartfelt psychic connections to other human beings, and the oft-ignored core of our awareness that is normally concealed from us by our nearly constant mental chatter.

The archaeological record suggests that the ancient Maya also employed such psychoactive substances, even though their contemporary descendants do not show much interest and their use is extremely uncommon. Early Maya left behind hundreds of stone mushroom figures, suggesting the existence of a spiritual practice surrounding these potentially illuminating fungi. Not surprisingly, these mushroom stones have been found at the very same early archaeological sites where the culture's greatest advances took place along the Pacific piedmont. Further reinforcing the possibility that the ancient Maya used hallucinogens, an image of the DMT-producing cane toad (*Bufo marinus*) was found at the early site of Izapa, a place closely linked to development of their intricate calendar traditions.

By 1976, the Ohio woods and fields of my childhood had all been bulldozed for housing and road construction projects, and the ponds where frogs once serenaded us as children had been filled and covered with lawns and look-alike homes. My father's death process had provided a virtual preview of my own mortality, pushing me irresistibly to explore life in earnest. I had witnessed political madness from both the left and the right, forcing me to search deeper to discover my own inner compass. I had read the mind-expanding fiction of Carlos Castaneda and was intrigued by tales of his exploits with Yaqui teacher Don Juan. I had been blessed with a radiantly beautiful and genuinely loving girlfriend, and some lessons from psychoactive allies had shown both of us that life had far more to offer than our culture had led us to believe. By the time we arrived in southeast Mexico in February 1977, we had already experienced numerous medicine journeys; but even these impactful revelatory sessions had not provided even an inkling of the far more radically transformative breakthroughs that were awaiting their precise karmic moment in the sacred lands of the Maya to inform our beings.

Without knowing it, life's circumstances had swept life's road clear in front of us and we intuitively sensed that it was time to start out on the next stretch of our journey. We gathered the bare essentials in our rather primitive backpacks and headed south for three months of adventure in the backcountry of Mexico, wandering from village to village in various native communities without even a clue that our lives were about to turn in a permanently and fundamentally altered direction.

Waking Up Among the Maya

Our first footsteps on the Mayan path came during a sunrise hike to the mystical ruined metropolis known by the ancients as Lakam Ha', or "Big Water." Lakam Ha'[1] is an exuberantly verdant Mayan archaeological site perched at the foot of a rugged, rainforest-covered mountain ridge. Gentle crystal-clear streams gurgle from under the lush jungle canopy and then course between 1,400-year-old temples intricately sculpted from finely textured limestone. The mineral-laden waters spill gracefully over wildly contoured waterfalls before pouring out upon the moist green savanna and continuing northward toward the vast marshlands of Tabasco and the Gulf of Mexico beyond. This enchanting city's original name, Big Water, probably came from its magnificent view of these extensive wetlands but it may have also referred to the site's own abundant and irresistibly inviting waters. Lakam Ha''s sparkling cascades, adorned with luxuriant tropical foliage, have carved magnificent natural bathing pools into the organic bedrock that were truly worthy of the city's ancient lords. More than seven feet of annual rainfall nourish this liquid realm where the nearly constant moisture silently floats heavenward in willowy white plumes that seem to emerge like magic from the living jade-green of the luxuriant forest.

In the areas where the tropical hardwoods have been cut down for grazing livestock, the moist conditions in the rainy season are perfect for the growth of *Psilocybe cubensis,* a large mushroom fond of composted cattle dung. My girlfriend June and I had been in the area for almost a week, staying in a tiny *posada* on the fringes of the Mexican town nearest to the ruins. Each misty morning, we wandered the hilly pastures in the morning, searching for the raw mushrooms that were to guide us, weeping for our shortcomings and sorrows, and taking heart in the discovery of our underlying capacity for genuine kindness and humor, toward the deep understanding that conscious and committed lives require.

I knew almost nothing about the Mayan world at that time, but with my father's recent demise as a harsh reminder of my own "impending" death, our physical removal from almost all of our familiar northeast Ohio cultural underpinnings, and a near total disillusionment with the direction of my own country, I was ready for a fundamentally new path in life. Without realizing it, I had come to my own crossroads.

Fittingly, my initial steps on to Mayan trails came on the day known as E'[2] in their sacred 260-day ritual cycle, a chronological system still used by the *ahq'ihab*,[3] the initiated calendar priests and spiritual guides of the Mayan highlands farther to the south in Guatemala. These interpreters of time also associate this day with the word *be*,[4] one's "road" in life. The revered calendar specialists and their ancestral Mayan predecessors have been meticulously counting the days in their holy *cholq'ih*,[5] the "count of suns," for more than two millennia. They link this day—one of twenty archetypal signs that function somewhat like a Mayan "horoscope"—to life's journey, to travel, to clearing one's path, and to the itinerant merchants who carried their burdens of cacao and other precious commodities along the snaking mountain trails of ancient Middle America. From the perspective of Mayan daykeeping, it was an auspicious day for initiating my journey on a path that has evolved into a profound love for Mayan ways and a keen interest in 13 Pik, the highly anticipated day in 2012 derived from their ancient Long Count calendar.

My twenty-two-year-old travel companion, June, now my wife of more than thirty years, had been coaxed awake this particular day by the melodious calls of tropical birds. She whispered that she had an overpowering feeling of delightful anticipation. She seemed barely able to contain herself, predicting with uncharacteristic certainty that somehow this was going to be the greatest day of our relatively young lives. Her intuition told her that something radically transformative was about to occur, but she had no inkling as to what it might be. After first tending to our rapidly growing collection of chigger bites, we headed into town. I listened to more of her exhilaration over a tall glass of freshly squeezed orange juice prepared by a kind elderly Mexican woman at an outdoor stall near the town market that was just beginning to stir. I was oblivious to the momentous life-altering changes that awaited us mere hours away as we headed out for yet another morning stroll in the cow pastures.

At midmorning we found ourselves relaxing against the smooth trunk of a colossal tree that crowned a grassy knoll some five miles from the Lakam Ha' ruins. As I scanned the southern horizon while scratching at my countless chigger bites, my eyes drifted to the partially mist-hidden Don Juan Mountains that rise behind the archaeological site. The exquisite site, considered by many to be the most striking in the entire Mayan world, had once been the richly ornate capital of the Classic Period city-state known simply as Bakal, or "Bone," ruled in the seventh century by its fabled lord, K'inich Hanaab' Pakal. For the ancients, the name "Bone" probably was a graphic and readily understood reference to death and the realm of their deeply revered ancestors. Since the kingdom was at the far western edge of the Classic Mayan world, a place where the Lord Sun, K'in Ahaw, "died" each evening, falling below the horizon, Bakal also had powerful associations with the blackness of night, the underworld known as Xibalba, and the inner realms of the human subconscious.

The sun was still rising from its nightly voyage beneath the surface of the Earth. As my gaze involuntarily shifted upward from the rainforest-blanketed mountains toward the sun, I gradually became aware of extremely subtle, randomly swirling patterns of faint light in the sky above the ruins complex. I felt confused when I found myself inexplicably incapable of focusing my vision in the strangely shifting illuminated area, as if a small portion of my field of sight no longer provided an image my brain could accurately maintain and interpret.

"Can you see that? What's going on in the sky?" murmured June.

As we stared in incredulity, a barely perceptible shaft of light appeared to come down from the sky and envelop us in its delicate golden hue. As a dedicated skeptic at heart, I assumed in the moment that I was finally experiencing the first actual hallucination in all my experiences on so-called hallucinogens. Gently bathed in this faint glow for just a few seconds, in a clearly defined moment, we simultaneously and unexpectedly "clicked" into a radically reorganized mode of perception. At that precise instant, with the light patterns now faded from view, we both shifted into a profoundly enhanced state of awareness that neither of us had even imagined possible. To this day, I cannot explain how it happened though it seems related to the spiritual field and realities within which the Maya live. My thinking became instantly coherent. I suddenly and effortlessly understood my life experience thus far with poignant clarity. At the same time, my relationship to our physical surroundings took on an immediacy I had never previously even imagined. To our utter surprise and profound delight, we felt as if we had finally awakened from a lifelong slumber and that we were some of the last to have finally opened our eyes. With reflexive awe and unavoidable humility, for the first time in our young lives, we tasted an overwhelming compassion that included profound sorrow and genuine ecstasy, a state I would later read about in the words of mystics from around the world. The full power of this deeply revealing and utterly fearless state of consciousness lasted for about three weeks and we both cried as we noticed it fading.

Even so, those few weeks thoroughly enriched and shaped our lives by placing our feet firmly on our own *saq be'*, the sacred "white/ clear road" of inner development. On that fateful day, our own life path had taken us to intersect with the roads first laid down by the ancient Maya and still maintained by many of their living descendants. Now, more than three decades after this radical awakening and approaching the much-anticipated year 2012, June and I have still only rounded the first few bends on this profoundly satisfying journey, but even our first rather tenuous footsteps on this path have led us to an ever-deepening life experience that combines extremes of both joy and grief along with an ongoing and reflexive appreciation for our existence, states that neither of us had previously known.

From the first moment of our personal "awakening"—and it *was* an instantaneous event rather than a gradual shift—several dimensions of this temporary illumination became unmistakably apparent. Even though the full intensity of this inner state proved temporary, we still had been fundamentally and permanently enlivened, both physically and psychologically. Our physical senses had become far more acute and answers to lifelong questions poured forth effortlessly in automatic response to each inquiry posed by our yearning minds. It became transparently obvious that every instant of our lives prior to this point had formed part of a perfectly coherent whole that had now culminated in this drastically heightened awareness. Each person in our lives and every experience, both the most bitter and the most ecstatic, had been essential and integral for this awakening moment. We knew that our personal life dramas had arisen from an ongoing process of unfolding consciousness that poured forth from the heart and consciousness of each being in synchronicity with terrestrial and cosmic processes infinitely beyond our capacities to comprehend. There had not been even the tiniest mistake in our lives, nor even one wasted second, nor could there ever be. Every single moment had contributed to who we had now become.

The fact that our initiation into this heightened awareness had happened for both June and me simultaneously revealed an awesomely complex intermingling and bonding of our two spirits that neither of us could have previously comprehended. Our marriage became a foreordained afterthought. We understood ourselves clearly as relative latecomers to a more fully integrated collective consciousness that had been shared by humans in countless generations since the origins of our species. I laughed to myself, finally "getting" that all of my prior concepts concerning God and the divine had been so pathetically limited. I had never understood religion or spirituality because I had no inkling whatsoever as to what people were referring to. I had never realized that conceptual knowledge of divinity was virtually meaningless when faced with even a mere glimpse of its actual grandeur. Sadly, I could see that, in many ways, religion itself often formed the most powerful obstacle to direct awareness of holiness and wholeness. On a tiny Mexican hilltop, for the first time in my life, I had become at least partially aware of my infinitesimally small, yet indescribably enchanting, role in boundless creation. June and I directly experienced ourselves as integral to the natural world and bound by a heart connection to all humanity. Because this new consciousness first came to us in the Mayan world, it is no wonder that our lives feel especially connected to theirs.

This totally unexpected radical awakening under a tree on the Mayan day of the "road" offered us a tiny taste of the knowledge and bliss we had been fervently searching for subconsciously for our entire lives. Ironically, and humorously, it also dramatically heightened our knowledge of the seemingly endless depths of our ignorance. Just this minute inner glimpse into the vastness and infinite complexity of cosmic processes allowed by our all-too-temporary "enlightenment" left us intensely awestruck. Truly, I thought to myself, the leaf-cutter ants we could see laboring on their tiny trails in the vegetation at our feet had a far better chance of understanding the intricacies of modern human society than we humans did of even beginning to comprehend the faintest outlines of the limitless universe in which we live. This direct realization of our incomprehensibly profound ignorance in the face of the divine brought with it a profound sense of relief and unprecedented satisfaction. After only our first tenuous steps on the Mayan path, we had come upon a surprising yet somehow sublime reinterpretation of the old adage, "Ignorance is bliss."

As my beloved girlfriend and I continued our hike on that auspicious morning, we discovered that our newfound clarity allowed our spoken words to flow with astonishing fluidity, heightened creativity, and newfound eloquence. Before long, we came upon some Spanish -speaking townspeople waiting for a bus along a paved two-lane road, and naturally we stopped to greet them. Although I had studied

Spanish for many years in school, my real-world language skills had remained awkward and hesitating. Now, as I addressed the family on the side of the road, I was shocked, and then overjoyed, to hear Spanish flow from my lips as if it were my first language. The intermediary translation process in my brain had simply vanished. Everything I had ever learned in my years of studying the language was now suddenly and effortlessly available for my use. Even more striking was our almost overwhelming sense of love. It was as if, upon making eye contact with these people, we instantly had access to the most essential aspects of their beings. We, of course, knew none of the informational details of any individual's life experience; but we did somehow know the results of those events in terms of their personalities' core qualities and we could not help but feel such an overpowering compassion that I was almost moved to tears as we wished each other well with calls of *"Que les vaya bien."*

The Mayan path took more literal form for us just an hour later on that same day. Still in the rapture of our radically enhanced state of awareness, we paid our ruins entry fee to a sweetly smiling guard and, with quiet reverence, entered the grounds of the ancient stone city of Lakam Ha'. Almost immediately upon entering the site, a Mexican man in his thirties, apparently a guide, approached us and asked matter-of-factly in Spanish, "How long have you been like this?" "Just since this morning," I replied, somehow not surprised in the least by his inexplicable knowledge of our inner state and simultaneously cognizant that he shared our awareness. "Come with me, then," he said as he turned and led us toward the edge of the towering rainforest. We followed without question, elated by the prospect of this unexpected adventure while reveling in the absolute fearlessness inherent in our newfound way of being. Within moments, we came to a small stone stairway just to the side of one of the ancient Mayan temples. The young Mexican guide slowly strode up the steps, motioning for us to follow, and then led us for a few minutes on a slightly muddy trail into the welcoming cool air of the forest that was teeming with life. He paused in front of a diminutive limestone shrine, now in such severe disrepair that one wall had completely buckled. "Walk down the little stairway over there and then climb back out through the dark opening you see in front of us here." Even though we had never seen this young man before, we reflexively followed his command and made our way through the rubble and down inside a small chamber that must have functioned as the little temple's innermost chamber when Lakam Ha' was still a functioning city. We made our way across the tiny interior space in the darkness and then carefully up out of the crumbling limestone into the tree-filtered light, finding ourselves almost in the same spot where we had started in front of the temple and where our new acquaintance awaited with a broad, knowing smile. Inexplicably, the strength of our inner experience had intensified. "This is only the beginning," spoke the young man, an obvious reference to the day's overwhelming new awareness. "There is no final destination. There will always be more to learn. Just keep walking on this path," he concluded. He was speaking quite literally. He motioned into the tall vegetation farther along the small trail[6] that we had taken. Without fanfare beyond brief smiles and light handshakes with our newfound Mexican friend, we set off on our walk for the first time on a real Mayan path.

An hour later, we found ourselves covered in sweat, breathing hard, and still hiking on this narrow and ever-upward trail beneath the moist shade of the towering rainforest canopy. The walk had been quite challenging due to the slickness of the uneven limestone when it protruded out from the overlying mud, plants, and tree roots. As we stopped for a much-needed rest to catch our breath, we heard the faint sound of gently slapping footsteps steadily approaching from behind us on the rain-moistened stones of the forest path. In a matter of seconds, a barefoot and noticeably muscular middle-aged man, the first Maya we had ever met, quietly stepped alongside us on the narrow, slippery trail. He carried what seemed like a truly massive load of freshly cut firewood that must have been nearly as heavy as his own body. The neatly prepared bundle hung from a thick leather headstrap that he called a *tahbal* slung over his forehead, the weight of the wood partially supported on his lower back with taut ropes. With a mildly bemused look on his sweat-covered face, the man put out his hand and ever so lightly grazed my own, exerting only the slightest of pressure for several unhurried seconds. The subtlety of the physical contact between our touching fingers somehow seemed to offer each of us an instantaneous sense of one another. Upon briefly glancing into the man's eyes, it became transparently clear that he was also awake to an enhanced awareness similar to what my girlfriend and I had first experienced earlier in the day. He seemed both surprised and pleased that we both shared this inner state with him. After he resituated the enormous, tightly packed stack of wood still in place on his compact yet powerful body, the man's eyes motioned us forward and with an inviting smile of encouragement, he said simply, *"Koxla"* ("Let's go").

This Mayan farmer's simple act of welcome came on the first day of a lifelong journey on a path that has proven both humbling and inspiring. The lessons found on this ancient way have brought an ever-deepening appreciation of what some Maya call the "Heart of Sky, Heart of Earth," words used to describe the source of the living cosmos. This book arises from a genuine sense of obligation to share our walk on the *saq be'*, the "white/clear road" first cleared by the ancestors of our Mayan hiking companion thousands of years ago amid the misty rainforests, pine-covered ridges, and still-smoking volcanoes of ancient Middle America.

The overhead vegetation thinned somewhat as the three of us reached the crest of the mountain, allowing more light to filter under the forest cover. Spread before our eyes through the treetops was a lush valley, a brilliant swath of green stretching to the next ridge on the distant horizon. An almost iridescent turquoise-blue river glittered as it snaked across the luxuriant expanse of tropical trees and cornfields. We learned later that the river's name referred to the *max*, local spider monkeys still living in the surrounding forest canopy. Partway along the gleaming stream, my girlfriend and I could clearly see a collection of perhaps forty thatched-roof huts, some with the wisps of silvery smoke from cooking fires filtering out through the shingled palm leaves. As we gingerly made our way down along the muddy and precipitously steep descent toward the village, our walking companion began speaking a bit in Spanish, our common second language. He explained that he and his people were Ch'ol, a group of Maya named after the sacred garden space where corn is grown. After a few brief words of farewell and another extremely light touching of hands, the man disappeared off a side trail and we were on our own again, sliding precariously across patches of exposed limestone made slick by the seasonal rains and worn smooth by bare human feet.

After we spent twenty minutes scampering down the wet, precarious slope, the trail leveled out on the valley floor and we heard sounds through the forest that struck me as human, but unlike any we had heard before. As we came closer, I could hear that the voices came from a group of youngsters who were laughing and making a delightfully refreshing assortment of playful noises almost like singing birds. I realized that instead of walking straight to the village center as I had intended, we had mistakenly bypassed the community entirely and arrived upstream along the bank of the river near what was apparently a favorite swimming hole for the local Ch'ol children. The joyous sounds came from perhaps five or six naked little boys who were jumping blissfully off the boulders, one by one, into the deepest part of the crystal-clear waters that flowed through their tiny hamlet. The boys shouted out delightful calls that sounded like "Hu huuuuu" in animal-like, high-pitched voices between seemingly uncontrollable fits of laughter. As soon as I announced our presence to the kids, they scrambled over to us quickly with a genuine sense of excitement and curiosity. Their sparkling clear eyes and hand gestures urged us to join their play in the water. As we hopped in, sweaty muddy clothes and all, I noticed in the eyes of these young Maya the same sense of enhanced wakefulness that had been evident in the eyes of our hiking companion only minutes before. After several group belly laughs and an invigorating dip, we followed the little gang of boys so they could show off the soggy, odd-looking couple they had found to their families. As we came into the clearing where the village stood, barefoot children of all ages seemed to appear from every direction to join in the amusement created by their unexpected guests. Older sisters carried infant siblings on their hips and boys took their little brothers by the hand in order to get a closer look. The children's excitement and enthusiasm were infectious.

Our first impression of life in a Mayan settlement was one of extraordinary tidiness and harmony. Every house component and nearly every human-made part of the village had been fashioned from vegetation that grew naturally in the immediate vicinity It was a domestic space fabricated with precision and care from machete-cut poles, intricately woven vines, lashed palm leaves, and ax-hewn wooden beams. There was no trash of any sort nor was there any obvious metal apart from the gleaming steel machetes that men wore from their belts like swordsmen of old. We were surprised to notice that the overall effect of our first experience in the Mayan way of living was not one of culture shock, but rather, a noticeable sense of profound comfort and ease. In this radically different environment, far from our Rust Belt homes in northeast Ohio, we felt oddly at home in inexplicably familiar circumstances. This seemed to be the safest place I had been in my entire life. To this day, I still feel far more comfortable among Maya than I do in my own cultural setting.

At our noisy group's first stop, a young mother emerged from below the palm awning of her house, greeting us in Ch'ol with a tiny infant slung across her chest in a long, white cloth. The baby was earnestly nursing and neither the boys nor the mother gave even a passing thought to her exposed breast. As I scanned the tiny faces, I could not help but wonder if I had ever before seen such an exuberantly happy bunch of children.

The growing little crowd of children led us to the village center, where we joined a group of men squatting next to the ballcourt, site of the modern-day Mayan ball game, basketball. The home Ch'ol team was playing a visiting team from a nearby Mayan settlement where people spoke another Mayan language known as Tzeltal. As we watched, I noticed that this local Mayan variant of basketball had a special feature. The crowd would whoop and shout most loudly not after a score, but when a player with the ball found himself in a "trap" set by opposing players. Throwing caution almost literally to the wind, the desperate ballplayer would fling the basketball straight into the air apparently hoping it would land in the hands of a teammate. With the birdlike hoots and laughter of players and spectators filling the village center, ball possession eventually became reestablished and the inter-Mayan ball game continued. The concept of competition here was distinctly unlike any I had previously known.

We squatted down alongside some older barefoot men to chat as they watched and commented on the lively game from the sidelines. They obviously shared the same open manner that we had noticed with the sweet man we had met on the trail earlier and the laughing boys at the swimming hole. Unlike the non-Mayan townspeople, the Maya we met were already in the heightened state of awareness that we were in but they had no need for the mushrooms. Their inner state was a result of their lifestyle integrated into the natural world combined with a cultural and genetic heritage passed down to them from their ancient ancestors. The social atmosphere here was profoundly relaxed and unpretentious. There was no rush, nor was there any discomfort with silent moments in the conversation. I became aware of a subtle, unmistakably clear psychological bond between them, a shared consciousness that I might never have noticed before our hilltop awakening earlier in the day.

As the basketball game ended, one slender middle-aged man walked over and invited us in Spanish to his home in order to meet his elderly parents, saying that he thought we would like to meet them since they were the oldest people in the village. The wood and palm thatch dwelling was inspiring in its simple dignity. I noticed that regular sweeping with a homemade broom had smoothed the earthen floor of the one-room house to a polished sheen. As our eyes adjusted to the dark interior space we were met by the man's mother and father, who greeted us in Ch'ol. The lean and bright-eyed elders lightly touched our hands and then the woman endeared us to her by offering a song of welcome, accompanied by a simple dance step. Although I could not understand her words, I noticed that, with the sound of her soft voice, others in the family quickly stopped chatting and the group's attention turned immediately to the diminutive matriarch. Affection, pride, and reverence flowed from everyone's eyes as her soothing melody moved the room to appreciative smiles. Even on a return visit decades later, while holding her hands on her deathbed, I saw that her gracious presence still commanded the profound admiration of all those around her.

After speaking to us for a few moments in Ch'ol, the kindly woman motioned to us with her powerfully expressive eyes to sit on some homemade wooden stools in the corner of the room. She then brought over a clay pitcher and indicated for us to hold out our hands. She poured out a bit of mildly warmed water from the fire for us to wash and rinse them, the excess water simply falling to the floor. She then went back to her clay griddle to bring us an unexpected treat. In moments, we each held a bowl made from a dried gourd full of steaming beans along with fresh scrambled eggs. On another tiny wooden stool, she placed a stack of hand-patted tortillas covered with a beautifully embroidered cloth to keep them warm. The elder woman showed us how to crush some tiny round chili peppers with our fingers on top of everything and offered us some coarse salt for flavoring. Once they saw that we had everything we needed, they all excused themselves to let us eat quietly on our own. Realizing there were no eating utensils, we happily used our tortillas to scoop up the delicious contents from the dried gourds. Never had such a simple meal been so satisfying. As we gazed about the small and uncluttered space, I was struck by the quality and minimal number of material goods the family kept. A beautifully hand-woven net held a clutch of eggs. Ears of multicolored corn were carefully strung from the rafters where I saw several reed mats that would later be pulled down by the family members for sleeping. The elder woman seemed to have a special affection for my truly lovely girlfriend, speaking to her sweetly and repeatedly in Ch'ol, gently stroking both her cheeks, and making comments while playing with her earrings. As we said our good-byes to all the members of the extended household, my partner once again became the main object of the woman's attention. The elder's parting words seemed quite serious, perhaps some sort of blessing, so we asked for a translation. "She told your wife not to fall down in the mud." I could not help but smile at the simple, literally "down to earth" practicality of Mayan wisdom.

Making our way out of the village that day in the company of a small crowd of giggling Ch'ol Mayan kids, we began to sense a richer realm of possibilities for ourselves than our northeast Ohio upbringing had provided for us. In contrast with what we had seen in our own country, I saw here that humans could live and die while experiencing a naturally occurring satisfaction with life that I had never previously known even existed. Compared to people in the U.S. mainstream, these unassuming and friendly people had virtually no material possessions, yet they seemed infused with a genuine sense of wonder and calm fulfillment that arose simply by accepting what nature and their own hard work had provided. After just our first few hours among Maya, I felt an irresistible urge to learn more from them, to align my own life's path as best as I could with theirs and to walk toward a more vital and joyful way of being human.

The Living Mayan World

Generalizations about the Maya such as those made in this book are unavoidably problematic. The Mayan region's environmental diversity and turbulent history have led to an astonishing variety of human cultural expressions. There may be as many as eight million Maya living today, depending on whom you include, that belong to some thirty different ethnic groups, each with its own distinct language and differing customs. Real Maya may be some of the most diverse of human cultures. There are Maya who call themselves Hach Winik, "true people," living in what remains of the tropical rainforest and whose men traditionally keep their hair long and wear simple white cotton tunics. In highland Chiapas, Tzotzil-speaking women kneel patiently in front of their backstrap looms creating masterful, complex patterns

of brilliant colors that emerge from their abdomens like newborn beings of cloth. There are Mam Mayan potato farmers eking out a living
above ten thousand feet in the frost-covered heights of the Cuchumatán Mountains. There are Tenek Mayan women adorned like queens
with crowns of brightly colored yarn tending cave shrines in northeastern Mexico. In the Macewal villages of eastern Yucatán, barefoot
Mayan men dressed in white guard the sacred green crosses at holy
sites they have stubbornly defended with their lives for generations.
Tz'utuhil Maya in Santiago Atitlán tend to a lovingly adorned wooden
image of Rilaj Mam, a shape-changing deity who wears a Stetson hat.
Whether K'iche', Chorti, or Q'anhobal, the members of all these and
more than two dozen other Mayan ethnic groups share many cultural
traits but they also differ sharply in important ways. On numerous occasions in Mayan history, many of these groups have been adversaries
and have sometimes even gone to war against one another.

With so many individual and ethnic differences, any of my references in this book to Mayan ways might have literally millions of
exceptions. Please keep this in mind. In reality, when referring to a

Besides the astonishing cultural diversity that exists among Maya,
there is even more extreme variety in their current living conditions,
even among people from the same ethnic group. There are Maya living in the shantytowns of Guatemala City who barely survive by selling recycled junk and trinkets on its often dangerous streets. There
are Mayan university professors, landscape laborers, corn farmers,
radio announcers, and illiterate sages. Mayan men swill beer on the
dingy streets of Oakland, California, after a hard day pouring concrete
while other Maya offer prayers to the mighty *dueños,* the guardian
lords of the misty mountain peaks in the highest parts of the Guatemalan highlands. Still other Maya change bedding in Miami hotels
while others serve Corona beer to U.S. teenagers partying in Cancún.

With so many individual and ethnic differences, any of my references in this book to Mayan ways might have literally millions of
exceptions. Please keep this in mind. In reality, when referring to a
particular cultural trait, there may in actuality be far more Maya who
have abandoned or do not have that specific practice than those who
still maintain it. Mayan elders increasingly bemoan this serious loss
of culture. For the purposes of this book, however, in order for us

to imbibe as much benefit as possible from this encounter with the Mayan world, the fact that not all Maya live in the same way or that many Maya no longer practice a particular behavior should not get in the way of our learning from their traditions.

While increasingly rare, there are still individuals, especially among the Mayan elders, who have developed genuine wisdom and awareness derived from continuous interaction with natural systems, a lifelong sense of community, and a deep appreciation of the ancestral past. Numerous nonindigenous Americans have had their first face-to-face interaction with genuinely wise and richly experienced people while traveling among our continent's original peoples. In such circumstances, it is not surprising that there is a strong tendency for us to romanticize Mayan culture and to ignore the shortcomings and challenges faced in the indigenous world. Just because we have come to know Maya who seem exceptionally gifted and wise does not imply that all contemporary Maya share those qualities. While most Maya delight in their children, respect their elders, and appreciate the life-giving sustenance of the natural world, there are many who do not. Focusing on some of the healthiest and most enlivening aspects of Mayan culture does not mean there are not Maya who are deeply troubled souls. Nor should it take attention away from the very serious problems that currently exist in the Mayan world. For example, in spite of the recent expansion of nondrinking evangelical Christianity among the Maya, alcoholism still takes a heavy toll in many communities. In some parts of the Mayan world, an intense combination of fear and mistrust has frequently led to extreme forms of communal justice with lawbreakers mercilessly killed in public lynchings. Spousal abuse, usually alcohol-related, is all too common in many parts of the Mayan world and I have even known some Mayan parents to be cruel with their children. As with human populations all over the planet, there are Mayan adulterers, murderers, thieves, and all sorts of other deeply troubled individuals. We must be careful not to romanticize away such innumerable and serious problems. Still, after fully acknowledging the existence of the many serious challenges and shortcomings in the modern Mayan world, we can concentrate our attention on the numerous Mayan cultural patterns and Mayan people that have so much to offer us in this era of 2012.

It is also important to recall that many of the cultural attributes described here in connection with the Maya are ones practiced by indigenous peoples in many other parts of the world, elsewhere in Mesoamerica in particular. Humans in widely different geographic settings have independently arrived at some similar time-tested conclusions in terms of how to live their lives best. The Maya represent merely one cultural expression of indigenous knowledge, one that is especially accessible to those of us living in the United States due to our geographic proximity as well as to the large number of Maya dwelling among us.

In spite of the rapid pace of cultural change and the numerous problems that exist in the Mayan world during the era of 2012, much remains that can help us in our current time of societal crisis. The cultural brilliance of the Maya now takes more subtle and sometimes surprising forms than those in its distant past. It shines in the joyfully excited face of a little girl admiring the multicolored beauty of shining corn kernels as she peels off the ear's dried outer leaves. It reverberates in the shamanic cadence of a Mayan evangelical preacher speaking of the coming apocalypse. It reveals itself in the complex brocade innovations in the ingenious weaving of a young female schoolteacher. It resounds in the emotion-filled voice of a Mayan university graduate student reciting the ancient creation story in the *Popol Vuh*. It shines in the eyes of a young boy in a remote Mayan village in Belize as he laughingly dances to the music coming from a neighboring Pentecostal church under the delighted gaze of his smiling traditionalist father. The common spirit sparkling in the faces of these contemporary Maya offers us hope and direction for resolving our own dire problems in the years preceding 13 Pik and beyond. More than one hundred generations of Mayan experience certainly offer a wealth of ancient wisdom.

CHAPTER 3

Cherish the Babies

K'iche' Mayan mother with baby in Momostenango.

Birth Mothers and Mayan Midwives

If we in the modern Western world were limited to learning just one thing from the living Maya, I hope that would be to truly understand how they treat their newborns and infants, the precious "sprouts" that have emerged from Mayan wombs into the human experiences much as the holy corn grows toward the sun from the earthen matrix. Maya recognize that these tender "green" beings, like brilliantly verdant young corn shoots, are quite sensitive at this early stage and require special nurturing to grow to healthy maturity. Both babies and young corn require protection from the sometimes harsh "winds" of life. Both newborns and sprouting corn need life-giving moisture in the form of rain or breast milk. Both live in a symbiotic relationship with their environment: corn's root systems protected by broad leaves of squash and nourished by nitrogen-fixing beans, the babies sheltered in handwoven textiles next to their mother's bosom while absorbing vital nutrients. Both babies and corn are completely dependent on human beings for survival; human newborns are so reliant on their caretakers that they would die quickly without help, and corn cannot seed itself without assistance from farmers.

The patient devotion of Mayan mothers to their babies is so evident that it strikes even short-term visitors to the region, just as it did on the first day June and I walked into the Mayan world several decades ago. Mayan women instinctively nurture their newborns and babies in ways that lead to fundamentally content, calm, playful, and well-adjusted children. The radiantly smiling and lovingly adorned kids who are the norm in most Mayan communities are living testimony to the success of the Maya's time-proven approach to child-rearing based on deep respect for the birthing mother, the baby, and nature's instinctive ways.

Mayan mothers' intensely intimate approach to raising children begins even before birth. The K'iche' Mayan activist and Nobel Peace Prize laureate Rigoberta Menchú said that in her own community, women consciously communicate with their unborn children, beginning an early "dialogue" of feelings that merely shifts locale after birth. During pregnancy, Menchú says:

> The mother introduces her baby to the natural world, as our customs tell her to. She goes out in the fields or walks over the hills. She also has to show her baby the kind of life she leads, so that if she gets up at three in the morning, does her chores and tends the animals, she does it all the more so when she's pregnant, conscious that the child is taking all this in. She talks to the child continuously from the first moment he's in her stomach ...[1]

The culturally encouraged creation, development, and maintenance of this powerful psychological bond between mother and child form the core of Mayan childrearing practices. This primary bond to the birth mother is the basis for the infant's later participation in an expanding web of secondary connections to its extended family and community, to the natural world, and ultimately to cosmic processes. Whereas the human animal is so resilient that we can often compensate for the generalized inadequacies in our birthing practices, there is no doubt that firm establishment of these psychobiological connections can greatly facilitate weaving of the broader web of consciousness that can ultimately lead to profound levels of human satisfaction while living in physically and emotionally challenging conditions.

Sadly, precisely because of these challenges, Mayan mothers and children have higher mortality rates than those in more developed countries. That does not mean, however, that Mayan birthing practices themselves are flawed. Maya suffer from high mortality rates in almost all areas of public health, not just in relation to childbirth. These difficult circumstances are due primarily to their extremely humble economic resources and the virtual impossibility of gaining access to modern emergency medical services. Until relatively recently, for example, the Mayan community I know best had almost no modern health services at all in an area where nearly thirty thousand people live. Nearly all births take place at home and the overwhelming majority occur without much ado. However, in the rare case when there are complications, the results can be fatal for both mother and child. One Mayan midwife I know has successfully delivered some 1,500 infants but she still tears up when she speaks of the one still-born who, from her description, sounded as if it could have died as a result of a prolapsed umbilical cord.

Even without access to adequate emergency medical backup, Mayan mothers have several advantages over our own expectant mothers. One of these is their relatively young age, even though such a statement runs contrary to our modern ways. It is the norm for Mayan women to have their first child before the age of eighteen and almost none have their first baby after age twenty-five. In the developed world, we typically consider becoming a mother at such a tender age to be highly unfortunate, grossly irresponsible, or worse. We feel it's vital that a couple wait to have a child until after firmly establishing the baby's future economic security. We also assume that a teenage mother lacks the necessary maturity to raise a child. Our own culture's beliefs do not take into account that the young Mayan mother gives birth integrated into a lifestyle that in many ways promotes outstanding physical health. She is constitutionally strong, flexible, and fully capable of meeting the energetic demands of both pregnancy and infancy. For Maya, the requisite maturity for raising children comes about naturally through meeting life's challenges rather than through the mere passage of years. Instead of waiting to have children as we do for the development of sufficient maturity, Mayan women instead actually become fundamentally more mature at an earlier age as a direct consequence of motherhood. In particular, Mayan women instinctively and effortlessly learn to put another person's well-being in front of their own, one of the principal steps in the human maturation process.

Expectant Mayan mothers also enjoy the advantage of far greater psychological preparedness for giving birth and providing infant care. Most have already witnessed a human birth, often on several occasions. Mayan birth usually takes place in her own home and so, even if a young woman has not directly witnessed the birth of her own siblings, she has become keenly aware of how the process works and how demanding it can be. Furthermore, she has witnessed the birth of dozens of household animals and, through these experiences, has acquired direct practical understanding and appreciation of the potentially life-threatening challenges that await her in childbirth. These Mayan prenatal "classes" arise as an ongoing part of a girl's upbringing. A young Mayan woman ready to give birth for the first time already has a solid, reality-based grasp of the birth process and a clear understanding that pain, or at least extraordinarily intense physical sensation, is an expected, normal, and accepted part of having a baby. She will not be surprised by the experience. The typical young Mayan woman works strenuously, beginning before dawn, for the sake of her family's survival and she thus naturally maintains a relatively high level of physical fitness. She is accustomed to creature discomforts that both men and women in the developed world would find extremely challenging and perhaps even depressing. As the moment of birth approaches, in the familiar setting of her own home, with her mother and midwife beside her, she may be anxious, but she is genuinely prepared. With her richly experienced midwife gazing into her eyes, she can sense her ties to the ancestral mothers of her people, and her natural fears find their place in a vast human context in which she plays a role that millions have played before her.

Historically, Mayan midwives and shamans have been the primary guardians of their culture's ancestral heritage. Even in the ancient Mayan creation story as told in the K'iche' Maya's sacred *Popol Vuh* text, the first couple at the dawn of time was an elderly midwife known as Xmukane and her shaman husband, Xpiyakok. Historically, Maya have viewed both professions as sacred responsibilities bestowed on individuals selected by the wise ancestral spirits. Every one of many Mayan shamans and midwives I have known has told a remarkably similar story about how they came to practice their profession. In each case, a health crisis or trauma forced them to search for the underlying cause of their suffering. At some point in this painful struggle, the prospective midwife or shaman had a dream vision or visitation from ancestral spirits in which he or she received the intuitive gifts needed to exercise the profession. After this "initiation" experience, which generally takes place in the context of a particularly vivid dream, the individual began to practice with members of the community, marveling at the newly discovered abilities that had spontaneously arisen.

Among Mayan midwives, these abilities include intuitive knowledge of herbal medicine. Several midwives have independently described to me how, when their very first patient arrived, they found themselves instinctively drawn to particular plants that produced effective results. Likewise, during the birthing process, they spontaneously interact with their patients in ways that they are certain facilitate a successful outcome. It seems logical that humans would develop instinctual behaviors to facilitate healthy births as well as to utilize plants that promote physical healing. As with many other human capabilities, however, these skills do not activate unless circumstances such as those that still exist in much of the Mayan world require their application. The "gifts" of the midwives, though seemingly inexplicable by the standards of U.S. culture, are natural human abilities that develop when circumstances demand them and when the surrounding cultural paradigm encourages their expression.

According to the sacred *Popol Vuh*, or "Book of the Council Mat," the primal midwife Xmukane was "Grandmother of Day, Grandmother of Light."[2] She is the Mayan equivalent of Eve but with the gift of insight and without any forbidden fruit. Her wisdom, and that of her matchmaker-shaman husband, is so vast that even the Mayan gods must consult with them when trying to create the first humans. Mayan midwives today are the caretakers of her noble lineage.

In the past half century, respect for the male half of this ancestral pattern has dramatically diminished due, in part, to misguided efforts of some evangelical missionaries that have depicted the shamans as ignorant pagans or even as agents of the devil. More recently, the growth of consumerism and the shift from subsistence living have also significantly reduced the perceived need for these spiritual specialists.

Ministers and laypeople from some Christian denominations along with a variety of entrepreneurial types have taken the shamans' place, at least in the public domain, although many traditional practitioners continue their work clandestinely.

In contrast, the critical role of the midwife in Mayan life has remained largely intact since physicians and hospital care are still rare for most Maya and since the midwives' spiritual functions have remained discreetly in the private sphere. Due to the decline of Mayan shamanism, the midwives now have a privileged place as guardians of their ancestral heritage. Their lessons to us are some of the most valuable that Maya have to offer.

My own wife, June's, story below points to this vital role of the midwife during the birth of our own first child and the value she perceived in following Mayan ways:

> Undoubtedly, the decision to birth my children without medication was directly inspired by the Mayan mothers that I encountered on our travels. I had no idea of the intensity of the birth experience when I headed down that road, but I could not help but be affected by the absolute joy of motherhood that these women radiated, and I realized that nothing less was acceptable.
>
> Reflecting back, I now see that my first birthing was in itself a rite of passage into motherhood. It was a sacred event like no other. My sincerest gratitude is to my angelic midwife who guided me through this most raw, powerful experience. I am indebted to her for carrying me through the explosive waves convulsing within my pelvic bowl. She made me be present, as it was so easy to drift off. She actually slapped me hard in the face at one point and told me that I needed to "be here now. You are the one birthing this baby! No one else is doing it for you." I obeyed and succumbed to her authority and strength. She stood by me, eye to eye, breathing out three shallow, quick panting

breaths followed by one long inhalation, instructing me to imitate her. When I thought I could bear no more, I focused more intensely on her face, staring into her eyes, following her breath, feeling her steadfastness. The beautiful genius of this method acted much like a potent painkilling drug, distracting my mind just enough to allow my body's natural volcanic rhythms to continue unimpeded.

During the transition stage of birth when the baby was moving through the birth canal, the intensity of sensation reached a level that I can only describe as primordial. I sensed and felt a bonding with all mothers from across the planet from the beginning of time sharing the experience of going into the depths of pain and suffering to bear a child for joy. I was fine. All was well.

The pushing phase commanded enormous strength, much more than I ever thought possible. Then, our beautiful baby daughter was born. A girl! What a surprise! What a gift to behold! The energy in the room sweetened. Within seconds her tender body was gently placed on my bare abdomen. What came next is so special and so important to tell: the experience of a physiological, instinctual "bonding" that I felt all mammals must experience in a natural birthing process.

My baby girl lifted her head for an instant and gazed into my eyes. In that moment, a cascade of endorphins exploded within my being and I fell head over heels into a state of euphoria. I was swimming "in love" with her, my heart palpating, joy rising, bursting!

This euphoria connected me to her intimately and deeply in that moment. I knew that I would always protect her; I intuited her needs. We were physiologically "bonded" like other animals on this Earth that give birth. I was a powerful woman. I was a powerful mother.[3]

Mayan Birth

Mayan midwives have told me that the most significant obstacle to a successful birth is the expectant first-time mother's fear of the unfamiliar and uniquely powerful physical sensations during the most intense phase of labor. Just as in June's story above, they depend on the establishment of a substantive and harmonious relationship with the birth mother and frequently begin this process well before the expected due date of the baby. In some cases, the young woman even leaves her own family's compound to participate in household chores in the home of the midwife. This arrangement allows the expectant mother to develop a sense of trust in her older caregiver and at the same time provides an opportunity for the mother-to-be to make a "prepayment" on the debt of gratitude she will soon incur with the midwife. At the same time, the midwife can assess the mental and emotional state of her patient so that she will be better able to calm the young woman's fears more effectively during labor.

Evolution has of course led to a tendency in animal behavior in which females that are about to give birth seek out circumstances that favor the survival of the newborn. In the wild, this usually means finding a dark, private place, away from potential predators, where the mother will not risk attack when she and her newborn are so vulnerable. For the same reason, even domestic animals seek out dark areas where they will have uninterrupted privacy. Rare, for example, is the mother cat that will have her litter in the middle of the kitchen floor. Similarly, as mammals, we seek a set of optimal birthing conditions according to the dictates of our evolutionary heritage. Mayan midwives respect this legacy by assuring that the birth process is a private one. Births take place indoors and away from prying eyes. In the Mayan world, being indoors implies very dim lighting since most Mayan homes depend on candles or the most rudimentary of electric lighting systems, and windows in most homes tend to be very small. Midwives keep out unwelcome visitors, wandering household animals, and any other unwanted intrusions.

Cherish the Babies

From the onset of labor, the young Maya has a kindly, highly experienced older woman alongside her. The midwife's presence is like that of a gentle grandmother, and in fact, she often actually is a relative of the young woman, there to ensure the continuity of her lineage. The older woman holds the birth mother's hand, gently caressing her head, quietly assuring her that all the new sensations in her body are a normal part of the birth process, an event the midwife herself has experienced many times before. All of the midwives I personally know have had numerous children themselves, and the powerful confidence they exude based on that wealth of direct body knowledge cannot help but assure the young woman. Along with her calm and supportive demeanor, the midwife sometimes makes use of a rich repertoire of freshly cut medicinal herbs to facilitate the process when needed. Typically, birth takes place with the young woman on her knees or squatting, holding herself up using one of the posts in the house or holding on to a rope tied to a roof beam for this purpose. Her position, logically, makes use of gravity to help the child descend farther down the birth canal with each contraction.

As mentioned earlier, the lack of emergency medical care in much of the Mayan world has also led to higher mortality rates for both children and birthing mothers. Even so, the limited availability of pharmaceutical drugs and other interventions in the birth process, somewhat ironically, can represent a distinct advantage for birthing Mayan mothers. Without artificial sedation, the first-time Mayan mother is clearheaded and fully aware of every new sensation in her body as her labor progresses. She gives in to the birthing process, keenly conscious of all that is happening and far more able to control her pushing than our own mothers, who are typically numbed with various forms of anesthesia, often slowing delivery and leading to the need for medical intervention. With the encouragement and ancestrally based authority of her emotionally steady midwife, the Mayan birth mother is able to cope with her own fears and give in to the powerful synchronous contractions that move the baby gradually down the birth canal. There is of course no surgical cutting of the delicate lower vaginal membrane and thus birth mothers recover rapidly once their child has been born. Most importantly, once the child is in the mother's arms, pharmaceutical agents do not cloud the critical mother-infant bonding process.

I recall our friendly neighbor in Ohio telling me when I was a curious youngster not to pick up any of the kittens that had just been born to her cat. She explained that if I picked up the infant kittens in order to play with them, it was possible that the mother cat might not want them back. Her comment surprised me but I reluctantly left the tiny squirming fuzz balls next to their recuperating mother. My kindly neighbor was referring to the bonding process. As with many other animals, if an event interrupts the bonding period immediately after birth and the mother and infant become separated for too long, the mother cat will not recognize her own offspring and will let it die. In fact, humans are unique among mammals, in that we are the only species that frequently abandons its newborns and refuses to nurse them. Numerous studies point to the harm done to our newborns and their later development by our convenience-oriented and male-dominated birthing and childcare practices, yet they now have become largely normalized.

Mayan midwives realize that humans are similar to animals in regards to birth and that separation of a human mother from her baby can produce highly negative results. In fact, the most crucial aspect of Mayan birthing practices is its support of the bonding process between mother and newborn. Bonding takes place immediately after birth when the mother takes the child in her arms and they have their first face-to-face encounter. Research has shown that facial recognition on the part of the infant is an ability that is specific to the period right after birth. Knowing how critical this process is, Mayan midwives gently lift the infant directly from the birth canal to the arms and breasts of the mother. Our evolutionary heritage has provided us with an umbilical cord just long enough for this to happen without pulling on the placenta still attached to the uterine wall. Even after the infant emerges, the placenta still is providing oxygen to the child through the pulsating umbilical cord so the midwives are in no hurry to sever it. With eyes wide open, the Mayan baby gazes into the mother's eyes, listens to the familiar sound of the mother's voice, and hears the heartbeat it has known since its first moments of awareness. The baby instinctively begins to suckle at the mother's breast while inhaling the scent of the mother's body that will be a constant in life for months to come. After the establishment of this initial connection, Mayan babies rarely are away from their mothers' bodies during the first year of their lives.

It is worthwhile making a distinction between loving one's child and developing the powerful psychobiological bonds that can be established in the minutes after the birth process. Most all parents genuinely love their newborns and are willing to make extraordinary sacrifices on their behalf. Such love is real and has powerfully positive effects on both mother and child, and in turn has an uplifting impact on our society. However, the birth bonding process I refer to here includes these profound feelings of love, but goes well beyond them. Ideally it creates a virtual unity of awareness between mother and newborn. Within this dimension of shared consciousness, the Mayan baby's cry is rarely perceived as an annoyance. Instead, the bonded mother responds instinctually, assessing her baby's distress almost instantly, and responds reflexively with ancestrally based assurance. Among the Maya, no baby-rearing manuals are needed. We humans already have a full range of successful parenting skills within us but we can develop some of these latent capabilities only through their activation in the birthing process. The child who has successfully bonded with its mother, or any adult caregiver for that matter, can then repeat that process in subsequent bondings to its family, the surrounding community, and eventually to the physical world itself.

One of the most ignored aspects of the birthing process is its potential empowerment of women. Along with death, the act of having another human being emerge from one's own body is one of the most significant events any person can experience. The persistence of the midwife as a key figure in the Mayan community, even in the face of rapid societal change in virtually every other area of life, demonstrates the cultural centrality of birth. Many women who have given birth as most Maya still do, without drugs, report that the birth process enriched their lives profoundly and in ways that no other event could equal. As my own wife entered the most intense phase of labor she said she felt overcome by a powerful connection with birthing mothers across time and even across species, knowing that she was experiencing an event in the same way that females had since the dawn of time. The birth process is a unique rite of passage that transcends all others, but relatively few women in the developed world receive its benefits. Here, where men generally control the birth process, women lose the empowering aspect of birth. The use of anesthesia has become standardized and female dependence on mostly male health professionals is almost total. Even when the attending doctor is female, she often feels obligated to conform to the male-created birth practices. Instead of feeling empowered by successfully completing the most challenging of natural human acts, our young mothers learn that, without men and the assistance of drugs, they are weak and incapable. The blow is especially devastating since their insufficiency has taken place in the essentially female realm of birth.

In stark contrast, Mayan babies are in virtually constant physical contact with their mothers and other family members beginning with the moment of birth. Mayan midwives intensify this pattern of regular touching through a program of focused stimulation of the newborn using massage. Like other mammals, humans depend on physical stimulation in order to activate the nervous system, the reticular formation of the brain in particular, an essential practice for healthy neurological development. Mammals lick their newborns repeatedly and thus assure optimal function of the newborns' mechanical and mental processes. Maya achieve similar results with infant massage beginning shortly after birth. Besides effectively activating the nervous system, Mayan massage serves to break up tiny adhesions and stiffness in the baby's soft tissue that have developed as a result of the relative immobility of the womb. It also gives the midwives the opportunity to mold the flexible cranium of the baby into an aesthetically desirable shape, a cultural pattern that probably has its roots among the ancient Maya who used special boards to shape infant heads into what they felt to be an ideal form. Images of noticeably flat-foreheaded Maya are the norm in the ancient Mayan carvings, paintings, and sculpture. Most ancient Mayan skulls show evidence of deliberate cranial shaping.

In the mid-1970s, June and I were privileged to witness what may have been one of the last expressions of this custom in Lacanjá Chansayab, a Hach Winik Mayan village deep in the Mexican rainforest, that, at that time, took two days of walking to reach. Shortly after our arrival in the tiny community, we were taken to the home of José Pepe Chan Bor, a well-known Lacandon leader who was described to us as their *presidente*. He seemed genuinely enthusiastic to show us his recently born baby from one of his two wives. I saw that they had a tiny piece of flat wood covered in cloth strapped to their baby's forehead. When I inquired, concerned that the tiny infant might be ill, Chan Bor explained that the idea was to create a flat and elongated forehead so as to be especially handsome. I have never seen or even heard of this practice still being carried out anywhere else in the Mayan world and feel indeed fortunate to have witnessed a living Mayan link to the ancient Maya of the Classic Period.

Nowadays, the deliberate massaging of the baby's head by the midwife, however, may have further implications beyond mere cultural aesthetics. The cranium is composed of several interlocking plates of bone that allow for a tiny amount of flexion in the skull, especially important as the baby being born has to pass its relatively large head through the birth canal. Modern practitioners of cranial osteopathy have found that some patients lack adequate flexibility at these intersections, and that mobilizing these "stuck" areas can alter and improve the body's structural alignment. It may be that Mayan midwives, through their deliberate manipulation of the cranial plates shortly after birth, reduce or eliminate the baby's need for such osteopathic adjustments as an adult.

Massages take place in the muscle-relaxing heat of the household sauna, a small domelike structure; saunas are still the most common way of bathing in many Mayan villages. They sometimes continue for twenty days, a period celebrated as a completion of the first of thirteen such cycles in the Mayan ritual calendar. Maya call the saunas words like *chuh* or *tuh*, onomatopoeic terms derived from the sound of sprinkled water instantaneously turning to steam on red-hot stones. The sauna is a symbolic matrix, a warm and wet womb of stone and mud where baby and participating adults re-create their own *in utero* experience in the dark, cramped confines of the earthen sweat bath.

Even after the initial phase of its postpartum life, the newborn spends several months as a virtual appendage of its mother, reflecting the Mayan understanding regarding an infant's level of awareness. Our culture tends to view newborns as having limited sensory capacity and our relatively shabby treatment of them follows accordingly. The Maya see the baby as a human being at its most sensitive and vulnerable. A Mayan midwife was once commenting to me about the medicinal properties of one of the more than thirty plants she used in her botanical practice. She said that it was helpful in treating what she referred to in Spanish as the "evil eye" in children. When I heard the term, my heart sank a bit. Many non-Mayan residents of the region had belittled my Native friends to me, in particular calling attention to superstitious beliefs such as this one and I disliked hearing what seemed to be a confirmation of their disparaging views. However, when I asked the midwife what she meant by this malady, I was surprised at her thoughtful response:

> Roberto, we adults forget how sensitive the little babies really are. They are used to quiet and their mothers. Twenty days after the baby is born, we have a welcoming ceremony that marks the first complete period of a person's life. On that day, all the neighbors come to view the newborn. Of course, everybody wants to see the baby, and people naturally look at its eyes so they can get to know the new

member of the community better. This is too much stimulation for a sensitive baby. It gets excited and maybe even a bit scared. That is the "evil eye" and this herb can help calm the baby down.

What I had mistaken for a superstitious belief in a malevolent spirit turned out to be a subtle understanding of the delicate nature of the newborn human psyche. It is the business of the midwife to help others remember the newborn baby's extreme sensitivity.

Mayan Infant Care

The bonded Mayan baby is seen as a blessing and a source of joy. Every effort is made to keep the newborn happy. Nursing is overwhelmingly the norm in the Mayan world and it begins as soon as possible after birth, sometimes continuing for two or three years. In fact, I can't recall ever seeing a Mayan baby sucking on a bottle. Among Maya, there are no pacifiers, no baby formulas, no breast pumps, or any of the other artificial means we have devised to attempt to replicate what is one of the most essential of human activities, the direct feeding of our young. Volumes have been written about the powerful health and psychological benefits of nursing, yet modern society seems bent on eliminating this most fundamental practice. Mayan babies nurse freely day and night, cuddled up inside a carrying cloth that allows the mother to perform her chores while her little one remains in constant contact with the warmth of her body and the sounds of her reassuring voice. These circumstances mimic the baby's prior experience inside its mother, providing soothing reassurance. This postpartum "womb" experience is reinforced by the filtered light that comes through the mother's brightly colored carrying cloth, which is very reminiscent of the baby's pre-birth visual experience. The feeling of partial confinement inside the cloth completes the illusion of a virtual womb for the newborn in conditions similar to those of marsupials, which carry their babies inside their snuggly pouches where they can nurse as needed.

The Living Maya

As virtual appendages of their mothers, Mayan infants witness nearly all aspects of the human experience. In doing so, not only do they gradually learn the skills of survival, but they also acquire patterns of mental behavior modeled by those around them. While working one day with a friend in the Guatemalan highlands, I received a lesson from her in potato farming, but also in childrearing. She pointed out plant pests, described planting and harvesting patterns, and drew my attention to the diversity of potato types and colors. Occasionally, I would hear her exclaim and call me over to her so that I could behold a particularly beautiful and well-proportioned specimen. She handed the potato to me with a sense of having discovered a real treasure and I could not help but feel grateful that there are still people alive who can derive happiness from the beauty of a simple tuber. A few minutes later, I heard the tiny voice of the woman's granddaughter, hidden from sight behind several rows of hand-planted corn I found the little girl crouched in the dirt, her bright eyes beaming up from under some large, scraggly leaves with her hand tightly grasping something. "Look, *tat* Roberto," she said as she unfolded her tiny hands. "Look at this beautiful potato." How quickly and easily she had learned her grandmother's ways. The gratitude I felt earlier for her grandmother's joy in a potato now grew from realizing that there would still be people with such subtle appreciation in the generations to come.

One cold evening in a lofty corner of the Guatemalan highlands, I sat with a Mayan family near their cooking fire as we shared stories. Between tales, our attention turned to a toddler, a lively and especially inquisitive boy nearing two years of age. In homes without television or other forms of modern entertainment, and once everybody already has heard most of the traditional and family stories several times, watching the little ones often ends up being the best amusement available. This particular night, the youngest child in the family wandered around the small kitchen area with the entire rest of his family as his appreciative audience. The enchanting toddler first chased the dog out the door as he had seen his elders do, making some shooing sounds that delighted his tiny audience. The little boy then began picking up some strands of brightly colored thread that a cat was playing with on the earthen floor that came from some brocade work done earlier in the day for a woman's blouse. Threads awkwardly in hand, he stepped deliberately in the direction of the fire, where he apparently planned to toss them into the flames, one destination for household trash. As I reflexively started to get off my stool to stop him, I noticed that nobody in the room of extended family members seemed even remotely worried. No one, apparently, was going to stop him from getting too near to the fire. Since nothing else was happening, all eyes were on the youngster as he held out his hands over the flames to drop the threads clinging to his little fingers. Unable to shake them off right away, he let out a yelp as the heat from the cooking fire startled him into a tearful retreat to his mother's waiting arms. To my surprise, instead of responding with words of consolation, the little group, including the mother, burst into lighthearted laughter. My sense was that the humor was not mean-spirited amusement at the expense of the whimpering little boy, but rather, an innocent delight in seeing and remembering how we humans learn things most effectively, through direct and sometimes painful experience.

Later that night in bed, with blankets over my head for protection from the cold night air, I wondered about the wisdom of allowing a small child to risk injury from a heat source. The risk was quite real but I could see that there were also some definite benefits to my Mayan friends' approach. In contrast to the repetitive cautions we regularly give our own children about similar hazards, no words would ever be necessary in the future to warn this Mayan child about fire. Mayan culture understands that life itself is the greatest of teachers, especially in the form of "our Mother," a term used by Maya to describe the natural world. The humorous and matter-of-fact response by the adults to this little one's minor injury strongly assured the boy that he was not seriously hurt, thus speeding his emotional recovery; and it indirectly discouraged overreactions to minor pains in the future.

Such Mayan childrearing practices might sometimes seem alarming to those of us used to being on constant guard to avoid even insignificant potential threats to our children. Recently, I happened to be in the highlands after the corn harvest, which in some parts of the Mayan world is also kite season due to the ready availability of extremely lightweight cornstalks for building material at this time of year. While a group of young and old worked meticulously on their unique flying contraptions, a four-year-old boy decided to try out the shiny machete that he'd found lying nearby on the ground that had been used to cut down the few needed cornstalks. He grasped it firmly by the handle and started swinging it around wildly. I saw the glint of the recently sharpened blade flash repeatedly nearby as he whirled it about like a samurai warrior preparing for battle. If the scene had taken place in the States, nearly every person present would have intervened in some way, by screaming or quickly yanking away this potentially dangerous farming implement. But in this Mayan setting, I don't recall that anyone even took their eyes off the details of their kite-making. Although such unconcern might strike some as irresponsible, in the relatively child-friendly environment in traditional Mayan communities, parents prefer for their children to learn through allowing them to play fully at being an adult. The surprisingly precision usage of machetes by Mayan farmers and the relative infrequency of machete injuries in both adults and children are testimonials to the benefits of this approach.

Although Mayan mothers typically calm their infants by offering them the comfort of their breast, on occasion I have seen a mother resort to more extreme measures. In a time-honored technique more typically practiced by midwives and shamans, the mother sprays the baby with a soothing aromatic herbal remedy by pouring a small portion of the liquid into her mouth and then atomizing the liquid using her lips. As she expels the herbal infusion, she sprays this liquid medicine in a fine mist directly into the crying child's face. The explosion of coolness so thoroughly startles the baby that he or she typically stops crying immediately. Although the herbs used in this "emergency" measure probably have some sedative effects, I sense that its primary effect is to help the child break the cycle of out-of-control sobbing.

Just as adults get stuck in bouts of repetitive thinking, churning over thoughts like a skipping vinyl record, infants too can become consumed by repetitive behaviors that are difficult to stop without assistance. The spray of cooling liquid does no harm to the child, but the mild shock it produces seems to be enough to snap most babies out of their bouts of tears.

I recall a visit among the Tenek people, known to most of the outside world as *Huastec*. The Tenek live far apart from all the other Mayan groups in a remote area of northeastern Mexico not far from the Gulf of Mexico. Due to their proximity to the Texas border, I was regularly able to take my own young family there to visit when I was in graduate school in Austin. We were staying in a very remote hamlet that was several hours' hike into the mountains on a tiny trail. On one occasion, we stayed with a family who lived in a one-room thatched-roof house with a dirt floor so smooth from daily sweepings that it actually shone if the light was right. There were five small children in the household, one too young to walk. We joined the family that night sleeping on reed mats laid out on the floor. When I awoke at first light, the woman of the household was already preparing breakfast in a tiny adjacent structure where she kept her fire going through the night. As we got up, all the sleeping mats were rolled up and carefully placed in the rafters, leaving virtually the entire interior of the house empty and providing a pleasantly sheltered workspace for shelling beans, the main activity of the coming day.

Over the few days we stayed there, I developed a genuine sense of awe regarding the children's almost flawless behavior. Even though they curiously looked through every compartment of our backpacks, they took nothing and replaced things as best as they could where they had found them. They eagerly took my own children to explore the local "sights," especially the biggest trees, a locally revered cave with an unusual hole in the top where a brilliant shaft of sunlight entered, and the massive boulders that were their favorite play spot. As far as I could tell, the parents never reprimanded the children or limited them in terms of where they could go. In fact, the parents barely seemed to pay special attention to them since they were far too busy with work of their own. The woman of the house, still nursing her youngest child, was consumed with preparation of meals, tending to the household animals, and carrying water down from a tiny spring several hundred yards above them in the side of a limestone cliff. The man was digging postholes for a small corral he was making for the calf they had just managed to purchase. Their children were absorbed in joyful play and occasionally helping when able with household chores.

On the day before our departure, I could not resist asking our hosts what their secret was to raising such remarkably pleasant and well-behaved children. I complimented the man on their obvious childrearing skills and inquired about whatever special discipline techniques they might have used. After a few seconds of hesitation and a somewhat puzzled look, he replied, "We don't do anything. They just turn out that way." Although his simple answer was not at all what I had expected, I now see that his response contains the essence of the Mayan approach to childrearing. Ironically, given the extraordinary success that Maya have with raising children, they seem unconcerned with how best to carry this out. Instead they focus on the survival tasks at hand and trust in nature's benevolence during childhood acquisition of experientially based learning. Instead of worrying about how to be good parents, Maya rely on the powerful unspoken bonds that have been forged between parents and their offspring since birth, and highly successful childrearing unfolds without special effort or planning.

The promise of 2012 as a radically positive societal turning point cannot be fulfilled until we learn how to raise human beings who have both the capacity and inclination to adopt environmentally sustainable lifestyles and who enjoy unhindered development of more comprehensive states of awareness. Ironically, for humanity to enjoy a truly satisfying continued presence on our planet our approach must be rooted in the proven successes of the past, especially in the case of birthing more conscious human beings. Mayan birthing and childcare practices simply follow the natural patterns of other mammals and have existed since the dawn of our species. By remaining sensitive to our animal heritage, they activate evolutionarily shaped human developmental processes tied to birthing that have been compromised since the generalized implementation of unwarranted medical intervention. Given our current preference for constant personal comfort and for minimal exertion of effort, those wishing to follow the Mayan road must develop sufficient determination to resist certain aspects of mainstream medical culture that interfere with nature's ways, while at the same time taking advantage of current medical technology as a safety precaution for the rare instances when emergency intervention is genuinely necessary. The birthing practices of the living Maya are potentially their greatest gift to the modern world. The success of our efforts to bring about a positive turning point for our species in the era of 2012 will in many ways be determined by how we treat the newest and most sensitive among us, our babies.

CHAPTER 4

Weave Bonds of Community

K'iche' Mayan spiritual guides prepare ceremonial fire while visiting Santiago Atitlán.

Inner Connections

On the Saturday immediately following our initial awakening experiences in the Mayan community, we went shopping for fruit and vegetables in the weekly market in the then-tranquil town of Palenque, which has since become a bustling small city. Maya from the nearby Ch'ol and Tzeltal villages came to town every Saturday in order to sell their produce and purchase a few necessities. Starting out from their mountain hamlets before sunrise, men and women carried massive loads of cacao, chayote squash, and corn suspended from their heads using the ancient cargo-carrying strap still commonly used by many Maya. They hoped to get to market near sunrise in order to conduct business smoothly in the calm of the morning. That would give them time to mingle and gossip with friends and relatives who were in town from other Mayan communities. In those days few villagers wore shoes and fewer still spoke more than a few words of Spanish. For those reasons, racists among the Mexican storeowners in the market viewed these barefoot Maya as unintelligent primitives unequal to those of Hispanic origins like themselves, whom they called *gente de razón*, "people of reason."

While doing our best to choose a perfectly ripe papaya, our attention turned to a group of five or six Ch'ol men who apparently had finished selling their goods and stood lined up next to each other, leaning against one of the market walls. They did not speak to one another, but as I observed them more closely, I became aware that they were in reality highly attuned to one another. Through processes that I did not comprehend at that point, these men had developed sufficient sensitivity to allow them to share an acute awareness of one another. These Mayan men did not use telepathy in the sense that words passed from one man's mind to the others. Instead, I realized, communication between these Mayan villagers occurred on a far deeper and more intimate level than mere words. Their shared sense of awareness renewed itself occasionally through momentary eye contact. For this reason, I found out later, many Maya avoid more extended eye contact since a more prolonged interaction is intrusive and would enter into a level of intimacy reserved for only the closest of family relationships.

The bonds of shared inner awareness come about effortlessly in living Mayan communities that still practice traditional lifestyles. The individual psychological capacity for these profound interpersonal connections begins with the primary bonding between mother and child, and then is nurtured through the subsequent bondings to the extended family and neighbors that will be discussed in this chapter.

In the era of 2012, with our highly fragmented communities and split families, we have much to learn from living Mayan practices that are ancestral in their origins.

In at least one Mayan group, this community-enhancing capacity for shared awareness extends even beyond the realm of physical proximity. In his book on the Lacandon Maya of Chiapas, Victor Perera described his first attempt to meet with the late patriarch of Najá, Chan K'in, a man seen by many as the last Mayan priest uninfluenced by Christian beliefs.[1] Upon arrival in this tiny rainforest hamlet, Perera asked one of the other senior members of the community about the whereabouts of Chan K'in. The older man speculated that Chan K'in was probably out working in his cornfield. Unexpectedly, as the elder spoke, an image of the old Chan K'in appeared in Perera's mind and, sure enough, the famed Lacandon elder was out doing some chores in his cornfield. Apparently witnessing the same mental scene, Perera's host confirmed that now he too knew Chan K'in's whereabouts.

My own first experience among the Lacandon Maya suggests yet another subtle level of interpersonal communication, that of dreams. After hiking for three days in what was then relatively intact forest back in the 1970s, my wife and I were nearing a Lacandon settlement not far from the Usumacinta River. The first person we met was a middle-aged man with flowing long hair in the simple attire of all Lacandon males, a long, white cotton tunic. His words of greeting to us included a statement that he had been expecting us. He said he had seen our forms in his dreams the previous night and knew that we would be arriving soon. Although this usage of dreams may not be widespread among the Maya in general, its usage among the Lacandon is suggestive of the sometimes esoteric nature of Mayan human relations.

Weaving Community

When a Mayan weaver kneels on her *pop*, this mat symbolically ties her to ancestral community leadership and council. In an earlier time, she would have knelt upon a mat of woven reeds as in the name of the sacred *Popol Vuh*, the "council book" known literally as the "Mat Book." The reeds of her mat also symbolically tie her to the primal waters of the lakeshore Mayan world, highly esteemed places of abundance in nature. Customary burial for Maya often included interment of the person's *pop*, a remarkably lightweight and durable sleeping mat still used in some areas. Thus, the reed mat also recalls the ancestral *mam*, a term that refers both to those who have already passed into the realm of spirit and to the living community elders. In modern times, as we draw nearer to the completion of the next large cycle in the Mayan Long Count calendar on 13 Pik, the woman kneels on a manufactured pad of assorted recycled fibers that now serves as an unspoken reminder of the council elders in Mayan communities across several thousand years of history.

The weaver's backstrap loom stretches out in front of her and connects to a beam on the porch of her house with a taut rope. While her mat connects her with the ancestral Mayan community, the loom extending from her abdominal area and strapped behind her hips links her with the female creative power since her textile artistry emerges in front of her from just outside the womb. Both her babies and her weavings are creative products of her body's core, her *k'uh*, located in the middle of her abdomen. Use of the loom, particularly for the extremely complex brocade work created by some Mayan women, leads to the development of very high levels of physical dexterity in the hands. The fine motor skills required to weave a beautiful piece of cloth lead to virtual ambidexterity in many Mayan women as well as a well-developed ability to concentrate her attention for an extended period. These concentration skills provide the woman with access to a consistent sense of inner calm, very much as in the process of meditation. Through regular repetition, weaving becomes a dependable tool for calming frayed emotions or mental agitation. Good weaving also demands mental clarity since even a tiny mistake can require lengthy repairs.

Recently my wife and I reunited with a longtime Mayan friend from Guatemala. She and her extended family had welcomed us into their world many years ago but we had not seen her in her hometown for several years. Her life had been a personal variant of the struggle for survival common in the Mayan world. Orphaned at a young age, she had been raised by her loving grandmother. She found a hard-working husband, but after she had given birth to four children, he died from cancer at age twenty-eight. Since her own parents were no longer living and her dear grandmother had died, members of her extended family helped as best as they could. The woman began weaving intensely, eventually producing a small stockpile of extremely beautiful textiles for sale and barter. She managed to keep the fatherless family going while the children were small but her desire to provide them with an education beyond the primary school level eventually produced a dire economic situation. Only grade school is free in Guatemala. At the middle school level, although costs are minimal, they can prove restrictive for many Maya such as our friend. In order for her children to attend high school, they would need to live in a city two hours away and would need to pay for their living expenses there apart from tuition. In the midst of these increasingly trying circumstances, the tiny storage shed containing her precious treasure of weavings burned to the ground when an unattended candle set the little structure ablaze. In desperation and tormented by her desire to remain with her children, our friend decided to risk her life and travel to find a job in the United States to pay for their education. Only recently did we discover that she was living less than two hours away from us.

When I went not long ago to bring her to our home for a visit, she talked nonstop for hours about her trying experiences here in the United States. She lives in a very remote area in Florida and labors in brutal heat helping in the cultivation and packing of watermelons. She was familiar with hard work from her life in a Mayan village but found that the social dimensions of her experience here were overwhelmingly depressing. She felt doubly isolated. She lives entirely among Mexican migrant workers who mocked her because she is Native American, an all-too-common expression of the severe racism against Maya so prevalent in their homelands. The Mexicans who mistreated her were themselves isolated in a hostile land by the racism of the English-speaking majority. A world away from her children, her extended family, her community, and her culture, our friend found herself moving into deepening bouts of sadness. When she thought that she had reached her lowest point, she remembered how much she had enjoyed weaving at home and tried to imagine how she could set up her own makeshift backstrap loom. Rummaging through a neighbor's trash bin, she found some plastic rods from discarded blinds and a few wooden door moldings. In a nearby dumpster she was delighted to find a discarded broom. Using a dull kitchen knife, she cut the necessary length of wood from the broom handle and, with amazing ingenuity, she eventually assembled a loom capable of producing the complex ancient designs that her beloved grandmother had taught her as a child, all from household garbage. The loom saved her. Weaving brought back her joy in life, provided a creative outlet, and restored her inner peace. As she assembled her loom in our living room, she recalled how her grandmother had been so strict with her while teaching her to weave, even sometimes smacking her young fingers when she made mistakes. When I asked how she felt about this harsh training, she gushed into weeping expressions of gratitude, praising her grandmother for having given her this most precious skill that had rescued her from severe depression.

While the emotional and mental benefits of weaving are well known among Mayan artisans, the creation of beautiful clothing is most valued for its enhancement and acknowledgment of Mayan community. I once asked a Mayan friend why she continued to weave and wear her own intricately designed and brightly colored blouses. To complete one of these elaborate articles of clothing required between two and three months of intensely focused labor on her backstrap loom, not to mention the cost of the cotton thread and other materials. Factory-made blouses were available in the market just blocks away for a fraction of the cost. Wearing the handwoven blouse outside of her town risked exposure to the derision of non-Maya and, during the Guatemalan civil war, might have led to far worse. She replied to my question by simply explaining, *"Somos naturales. Es parte de nosotros,"* "We are natives. It is a part of us." She went on to explain that her blouse was an outward sign of her inner connection to her local community and her Mayan ancestors that she was unwilling to set aside. Too much was apparently at stake for her.

Her favorite color of thread was red, a preference shared by many Mayan weavers in the highlands due to its symbolic association with the heat of the rising sun and that most precious of substances, human blood. Blood, in turn, is a reminder of the common ancestry shared by members of each Mayan community. The ancient Maya felt so strongly about these vital bonds that they drew blood from their own bodies in rites meant to demonstrate their willingness to sacrifice themselves for the broader community and to establish inner communion with their blood ancestors. Classic Mayan temples depict rulers in the act of this ritual bloodletting. Men pierced the penis while women pierced the tongue, allowing the droplets of this most sacred of substances to drip down into baskets filled with paper made from tree bark. Participants then burned the paper, sending the blood offering into the ethers. Temple carvings show ancestral beings appearing out of the smoke, reestablishing blood ties between distant generations.

Working Together

Maya reinforce their ancestral community bonds through regular communal work projects. Work has very strong positive connotations in the Mayan world since their survival has been dependent on their willingness to work hard in often challenging circumstances. Except in a few areas where tourism has become overwhelming, begging is extremely rare among the Maya. The assumption is that if one works hard enough, a person can meet the basic needs of one's family. Only once have I seen a man begging among the Maya. He boarded a crowded bus in the highlands and went from seat to seat with his hand outstretched. I had seen similar scenes in Mexico on numerous occasions and admired how many people there would willingly contribute to the beggar's welfare from their own, often meager, resources. The busload of Maya reacted to the man quite differently. While my paltry abilities in Mam kept me from understanding the details, I distinctly heard repeated, and not very friendly, references using variants of the word "work" as they almost indignantly refused the man's requests.

Besides the basic purpose of ensuring survival, work in the Mayan world serves the purpose of maintaining and strengthening one's body. The daily routine of many rural Maya is often extremely rigorous. Over the course of multiple generations, such rigors tend to weed out the weakest, leaving a population that, in spite of living in poor economic circumstances and without access to adequate medical care, is often remarkably fit. I recall taking a nap in the shade of a tree one day next to some old temple mounds in the Guatemalan highlands. I awoke to the voice of an old man as he sat down to rest next to me. After exchanging some introductory pleasantries, we began to chat. He said that he didn't know how old he was, but I'm quite certain he was at least in his seventies. In spite of his advanced age, the man was in amazingly powerful physical condition. He had just hiked several hours over a mountain pass at over ten thousand feet in elevation carrying a heavy load. The musculature in his arms and calves was well defined and he sat with near-perfect posture. I commented to him that I did not know a single person in my own country who was in such outstanding shape at his age. He could barely contain his laughter. He said that he and everybody else nowadays were sickly and weak compared to how the hardworking ancient ones used to be. Even his own father, he said, was far stronger than he was and worked so hard that he was able to even carry other human beings on his back for long distances using the tumpline strap used for transporting heavy loads by all native peoples in Middle America.

Mayan children learn to value work at a very early age and develop an understanding of their interdependence with others. As children begin to mimic their parents' work, the adults encourage them by integrating the children's contributions into the family's common efforts for survival. For example, young children typically accompany their mother when she goes to gather firewood. Quite naturally, young children begin to pick up small sticks and place them in their mother's growing bundle of wood. Later on at home, the child recognizes the sticks he or she gathered in the woodpile and watches closely as the mother adds them to the kitchen fire. Eating the evening meal, the child directly experiences the benefits derived from the firewood and, more importantly, sees that the twigs that he or she picked up earlier have real benefits for the family. The child receives great satisfaction from directly experiencing the fruits of work and this satisfaction gets reinforcement on an almost daily basis thereafter.

Among adults, work also serves to establish and build bonds within the local community. Many civic projects, from trail maintenance to building systems for potable water, require large amounts of human labor. Before such a project begins, however, potential participants must reach a consensus of support. General agreement on a course of action is far more time-consuming than coming to a majority decision but Mayan culture's prioritization of consensus suggests that, from their point of view, this time is well spent. Civic projects most often involve all of the men of a community or neighborhood. The work itself is often demanding. I usually walk home with broken blisters on my hands. Even so, the pace is never frenetic and the men seem to spend as much time chatting as actually working.

I recall working on a road building project that required one group of us to carry large paving stones down a slope to where another group of men was carefully laying them into freshly mixed cement. With my ego anxious to prove that I was not a typical *gringo* but could do real work, I picked up the largest stones I could carry and hurried with them as best as I could down the hill. Even though most of the men in my group still ended up carrying more total weight than I could, I am sure that they must have noticed my exertion, especially my labored breathing in the relatively thin mountain air. After witnessing my frantic efforts, a few individuals made a point of catching my attention and kindly suggested *"Chebi, tat"* ("Slow down, man"). As I gratefully began to take their advice, I gradually noticed more clearly what was really going on around me. Yes, we were working hard and accomplishing something real, but that was not the only purpose in our toil. This was a time to be together, to reconnect with neighbors by sharing gossip, discussing the progress of their corn crop, and offering perspectives on recent events. These connections reinforce the primary experience of working together for the common good, a collectively recognized physical demonstration of community solidarity.

Maya often avoid actions and attitudes that run counter to the community spirit, especially ones that highlight the individual at the expense of others. When Robert Bruce lived among the Lacandon Maya in the 1950s, he encountered this tendency when he tried to give away a .22 rifle he had brought as a gift. In an effort to be fair, he said that he would give the rifle to the man or boy who could shoot the most accurately at a distant target. Even though the rifle represented a potentially prized possession, once Bruce announced that he would award the prize competitively, all refused to participate, none wanting to stand out relative to the other community members.[2]

Maya tend to put the interests of the community over those of the individual. This tendency became especially clear to me when my family and I were invited to participate in a ceremony marking the transfer of power in a tiny Mayan village in eastern Mexico. The entire community of some two hundred souls was in attendance inside the thatched-roof community house. Local friends explained to us that village leadership rotated on a regular basis from one household to another. Eventually, virtually every man would be the main decision maker. This method not only recognizes the commonality of those living in the community but it also tends to prevent abuses of authority. Everyone knows that any one of his neighbors could potentially become leader in the near future. If a leader treated a member of the community disrespectfully, he would run the risk of shabby treatment by the victim in the future when the other man might hold the staff of authority. My friends also pointed out that the leadership of the village was always in the hands of both a man and a woman since the man required the advice of his partner in order to behave in the best interest of all. Single men were apparently unfit for making crucial decisions for the entire community.

Emotional Bonding

Another contributing factor in the development of the strong sense of community in the Mayan world is the powerful emotional bonding established during periods of intense sadness or celebration. Not coincidentally, I find myself crying and laughing with far greater frequency when among Mayan friends than when in my own country. Numerous Maya have expressed to me the value of shedding tears and of laughter. The Q'anhobal Mayan author Gaspar González once told me that crying plays a key role in Mayan interpersonal relations since it allows for moments of genuine empathy. Sometimes this state is facilitated by nostalgic marimba music and alcohol consumption. Funerals in some Mayan communities sometimes include a period of deliberate wailing, a dirge that, in context, becomes contagious. The unrestrained expression of sadness, as an individual and as a community, is regarded as a healthy human norm and a natural means for easing one's burden and further deepening the bonds of family and community.

I first became aware of this on my first trip to Guatemala while I sat chatting with a family friend in her kitchen. The gradual approach of intensely mournful sobbing outside the house interrupted our conversation. Although I was initially alarmed, my friend was utterly calm and we went out to find an elderly neighbor in the midst of an intense bout of tears. My friend offered her a few words of consolation in her own language and simply sat quietly next to her grieving friend on a wooden bench. The older woman continued crying for another few minutes, leaning into my friend's shoulder a bit, and then gradually collected herself and walked out of the compound. As we returned to our chat, I could not resist inquiring about what had just happened. My friend told me not to worry. She explained that her neighbor's husband had died some ten years earlier and that the woman was still very sad at times and stopped over for a good cry when she felt in need of company. I could not help but be impressed with the ready availability of space for emotional expression and intimacy. In the years since this incident I have experienced many dozens of tearful moments in the Mayan world and have come to appreciate them as precious expressions of intimacy that add greatly to the richness of Mayan life and that often do not find adequate expression in mainstream U.S. culture.

Among the Maya, tears are a vehicle both for release and for interpersonal connection. My "worst" incident in more than thirty years of travel in the Mayan area turned out also to be one of my most satisfying. As I hiked along a highland trail one day along the river, I noticed a commotion up ahead. It was a wildly staggering man, crying profusely and yelling out angrily to no one in particular. As we were going in opposite directions on the same narrow dirt path, I had no choice but to pass beside him or turn back. As we approached one other, the man's attention became riveted on me and he seemed to become especially agitated. He lumbered toward me, yelling out words in his own language that I could not comprehend. Drawing closer, his arms started flailing toward me and I wondered if he was preparing to attack. As my adrenaline surged, I felt the man's arms around me. His body began to shake in unrelenting sobs. I had to hold him up to keep him from falling to the ground. Wrapped in each other's arms, I quietly told him that I could only speak his language very poorly. *"Nchyal"* ("My son") was his simple response. *"Ma chim"* ("He's died"). His uncontrolled outpouring of grief broke through my fear and pulled our hearts together. He had never had any violent intentions. He just wanted somebody to cry with and feel connected in his sorrow for the son he had buried just that morning. We now shared a profound connection in this sadness.

Mayan culture often seems to seek out ways to take advantage of this compassion that flows naturally from human grief to establish and fortify interpersonal bonds, not just between individuals, but also within the entire community. One day a young boy arrived at the home where I was staying with a message for me to go to an elder friend's house later that afternoon. This was a rare request and so, of course, I hiked down the hill into town at the designated time. My elder friend said that he wanted to take me somewhere special but, for some reason, when I asked where we were going he just smiled and said that I would see soon enough. I had grown accustomed to extreme hikes with this particular friend and so I was almost shocked when, after a mere twenty minutes on the trails, he said that we were almost to our destination. As we approached a small knoll I could hear odd sounds coming from above. They were human voices that seemed to be singing, but it was a song utterly unlike any I had ever heard before. As my friend and I walked into the family compound, I realized that the "song" was coming from inside one of the small adobe structures. Female voices seemed to be moaning in unison. My friend urged me forward, introducing me to those I didn't know in the small crowd that was packed together in the little dirt courtyard. As we finally made our way to the threshold of the house, I could see over people's heads that there was a group of four older women sitting on a wooden bench wailing in front of a man's lifeless body that was lying in a casket in the middle of the room. The horrible sorrow in their voices was a powerful inspiration for tears and most of the women's faces in the room were already wet from weeping. As we entered the cramped, dark space to pay our respects, one man handed me a small bottle of Quetzalteca, Guatemala's all-too-popular rum, offering me a shot of its warming and social-lubricating contents. Making our way through the tightly packed house and back out into the patio area, I was immediately offered a seat on a wooden bench with some other men. I made my best attempts to communicate with them in my toddler-level Mam, which they seemed to appreciate, but they quickly switched to Spanish so I could understand better. *"Nuhsama, tat,"* an older woman's voice said, interrupting our chat. To my surprise, it was the widow of the man whose body lay only a few yards away. In her hands was a bowl of steaming food with a pair of handmade tortillas fresh off the griddle that she had prepared for me. With the relentless wailing, the sobs of neighbors and relatives filling the space, the couple of swigs of liquor seemed to have an amplified effect on me and emotions welled up from deep within. Here was this lovely person, in the midst of her grief, lovingly fulfilling her duties as hostess of the wake, and taking the time to make sure I had been served. Her simple gesture of kindness made my eyes swell with emotion. Simultaneously I sensed my connection to the woman, her bereaved family, and all the neighbors mourning around me.

Bonds of laughter can be equally powerful since they produce deep-seated memories of joy associated with others. While there is much deliberate joking and clever wordplay among the Maya, such humorous moments of connection more typically arise in the course of daily events. One evening, friends invited my wife and me to a dinner in our honor not far from where we were staying. After a lengthy process of gathering all the guests, we sat down on long benches on either side of a string of tables that we had pulled together from around the household courtyard.

After prayers of thanks, the large containers of food began to make their way around the table. One of the main parts of the meal was what these particular Maya called *lita*. This humble tamale, plain steamed ground corn wrapped in a corn husk, is perhaps the most typical of all Mayan foods, appearing regularly even in ancient temple carvings as an offering to the divine. On my second bite my mouth virtually exploded with the familiar flavor and heat of an unexpected jalapeño pepper. Tears welled up in my eyes from the burning sensation in my mouth. As I recovered, I noticed a young man at the end of the table with his face slightly contorted, obviously having found a stinging pepper in his tamale as well. Before long everyone seated at the table was commenting on the hot tamales. One of the cooks volunteered that she had put the little "surprises" into the *lita* to add a bit of flavor, not realizing how hot they really were. Some people broke into sweats, others became tearful, still others made noises … but nobody stopped eating. With tamale tears in her eyes, our hostess joked that people there would miss us so much that they were all crying. Reddened, tear-streaked faces broke into contagious laughter.

The group could not control itself and entered into several minutes of unrelenting humorous release. Just as the laughter would begin to subside, someone would bite into another pepper and the reaction would reignite the hilarity. Such simple moments of shared mirth are as common as the teary expressions of sorrow and are just as effective in deepening the bonds of friendship, family, and community.

In this era of 2012, we can build on the firm bonds we establish with our infants to reestablish the integrity of our inter-human connections with others in our communities in order to minimize and reverse the effects of our atomized and deeply alienating social paradigm. By deliberately seeking out opportunities to work alongside one another, we become more comfortable sharing ourselves with our neighbors and begin weaving together the disparate threads that will eventually form a coherent and resilient community fabric.

CHAPTER 5

Revere Nature

Corn in Todos Santos Cuchumatan.

Mother Nature Is Divine

The ancient *Popol Vuh* recounts the story of the Mayan Hero Twins, known as Hunahpú (One Blowgunner) and Xbalanqué (Jaguar Deer). The exploits of these two archetypal beings, passed down in a K'iche' Mayan document from the sixteenth century, reveal a set of core beliefs held dear by Maya across ancestral time. The divine Twins were masters of the ancient Mayan ball game. They were capable of easily outwitting the immensely powerful forces of the Xibalba, the Mayan underworld, arrayed against them. Hunahpú and Xbalanqué almost effortlessly surmounted a series of supernatural trials supervised by the Lords of Death. At perhaps the most crucial moment in the divine drama, the Twins even defeated Death itself through an act of total self-sacrifice, deliberately leaping into the flames of the Death Lords' blazing oven. To make sure that the Twins were truly dead, the Lords of Xibalba ordered that the burned bodies be ground into paste, just as Maya prepare corn on the traditional grinding stone. Hunahpú and Xbalanqué proved to be immortal beings and returned as traveling acrobats to destroy Death itself. These all-powerful progenitors of the Mayan world outwitted every opponent and surmounted every obstacle in their mythic journey to prepare the way for the current age of humans made from corn. Only on one extraordinary occasion did they give way to a higher power, when Mother Nature herself imposed her ways upon the Twins.

Like the living Maya, the Hero Twins grew corn. Being virtually omnipotent, they decided to create two supernatural tools for their agricultural work. One divine Twin wielded an ax that could cut a tree with the mere touch of its blade. His brother created a large hoe that automatically removed weeds and prepared the soil. The magical ax and mattock did their work, and the Twins avoided the physically challenging rigors of mountain corn-farming. Hunahpú and Xbalanqué enjoyed the day relaxing as the magical implements readied the field for planting. The two feigned hard work in the field to their wise elder grandmother and midwife Xmucane, an embodiment of Mother Nature. In their efforts to trick her, they went so far as to rub dirt on their hands and throw sawdust on their heads as evidence of their labor. The following dawn, when they returned to their corn garden, they found that the forest had somehow completely regenerated and that there was no trace of their cleared field. After complaining to their patiently silent grandmother about what had happened, the Twins sent out their magic farm tools once again, clearing the patch a second time for planting. This time, however, they hid in the brush to see what would happen. In surprise, they watched as a congregation of every wild animal known to the Maya gathered from the woods and magically re-created the original ecosystem by simultaneously intoning a sacred incantation. The *Popol Vuh* says, "They are the ones who are doing it, all the animals, small and great: puma, jaguar, deer, rabbit, fox, coyote, peccary, coati, small birds, great birds."[1] At this point, the Hero Twins vainly tried to capture the animals but every single animal ultimately escaped their grasp, although some, like the rabbit, permanently lost their once-longer tails, snatched off by the Mayan heroes. The Twins eventually accepted defeat, the only time in Mayan mythology that they succumb to a higher power. Apparently, in Mayan cosmology, even gods must ultimately accept their integrity with other aspects of Mother Nature's plan, just as they do in childbirth.

The story reflects a widely held reverence among the Maya for the natural world that expresses itself in numerous ways. Traditionally, Mayan farmers make offerings and ask for the forgiveness of nature when clearing land for planting. Likewise, when deciding to cut a tree for a house, they do a ceremony out of respect for the tree, again asking nature's forgiveness for killing one of its creations. In the Lacandon Mayan community of Najá, traditionalists viewed the felling of the surrounding rainforest as a sign that the world would soon be ending. Such attitudes toward nature are common among indigenous peoples around the world, but in the case of the Maya, these attitudes may have been reinforced as a consequence of the environmental collapse that doomed the Classic Mayan world in the ninth century. The extended drought that decimated the civilization during that period arose from the population's overconsumption of trees. It seems likely that the Mayan veneration for the natural world was powerfully shaped by this devastating experience.

In extreme cases, this reverence can take on almost mystical dimensions. During our first visit in the Tenek Mayan communities of northeastern Mexico nearly thirty years ago, my wife and I decided to hike out and camp in a remote area lying along the forest-shrouded first ridges of the Sierra Madre Oriental. My teenage sister-in-law joined us in what was her first journey outside the United States. In the early morning, as we started out of the Mexican village where we were staying, a strikingly attractive older Mayan woman motioned to us from the edge of the narrow street where she sat on the pavement next to a small mound of squash seeds she had lying on a cloth. Tenek women have adopted an exquisitely beautiful way of adorning themselves, placing skeins of brightly colored yarn on their heads in the form of a crown and fastening them in place with strands of their own hair. Garlands of multicolored beads hung around the woman's neck, drawing attention to the intricately embroidered white shawl she wore that blossomed with images of flowers and patterns of stylized vegetation. Her bare feet, calloused from decades of travel on the mountain pathways, barely stuck out from beneath her folded black skirt. Since she spoke almost no Spanish and I had yet to learn even a word of her language, we attempted to conduct our simple transaction in silence using hand gestures and facial expressions. I wanted to purchase a substantial quantity of her lightly salted seeds in order to maintain our energy on the trail. She scooped the seeds up using a little bowl made from a dried squash and then carefully weighed them out with a simple balance mechanism that she kept at her side. Her asking price, which she repeated in Spanish, confused me since it amounted to slightly less than three U.S. pennies. Surely, this tiny amount could not be correct. Nevertheless, the exchange seemed to satisfy the elder woman, who smiled broadly as we nodded good-bye and turned toward the trail leading upward into the mountains. After just a few moments, however, the seed vendor's gentle voice called out to us and I left my wife and her sister standing with their backpacks in order to go back to the elder woman. She must have finally realized that she had undercharged us for the freshly roasted seeds that I now carried wrapped in the scrap of old newspaper she had used for packaging. I would gladly pay more to her since these seeds would provide excellent fuel for our bodies during the hike ahead. As I squatted down next to her, I held out a hand full of Mexican pesos so she could select the appropriate coins. To my surprise, she discreetly motioned away my outstretched hand and pointed to my empty hand, which I then held out to her. She scooped her little gourd into the pile of seeds once more and poured even more seeds into my outstretched palm, waving me off with yet another smile. This gesture of kindness was an auspicious beginning for the Tenek portion of our walk on the Mayan road.

My delightful interaction with the seed-lady soon faded from my mind as we strained under the weight of our backpacks to climb the surprisingly steep trail out of the village. Within a few minutes, we were literally drenched in sweat, wondering how long it would take us to reach the first ridge. After we climbed intensely for perhaps forty-five minutes, the trail leveled out slightly and we joined a small family resting in the shade. After lightly touching hands with the adults, I attempted to inquire about possible spots for camping. The man was only partly familiar with Spanish and politely asked his own questions in carefully measured words about our origins and intentions. He assumed that we were going to a place he called Golondrinas, or "swallows." I had no idea what he was talking about but he insisted that it was a place worth visiting and that it was a mere one-hour walk away. As we made our way along the muddy path, the vegetation gradually shifted, the trees gradually became taller, and the sound of unfamiliar birds more frequent. Up ahead on the trail I saw a man approaching, dressed from head to his bare toes in white muslin. He strode confidently toward us with a radiant look on his sharply chiseled face as if he could not wait to talk to us. After a brief touch of our right hands, he gestured broadly to us with his arms and spoke in broken Spanish. *"Miren,"* "Look," he repeated, pointing to the massive tropical trees, to an orchid tucked into a woody crevice, to the squawking parrots above, and then to the distant horizon barely visible through the vegetation. "It's all Tata K'icha [Father Sun, the supreme deity of the Tenek Maya]." He repeated his words with irresistible enthusiasm as if this were the most important thing we could ever know. According to this delightfully happy man, all of nature's bounty was the physical manifestation of the divine—not merely divinely inspired creation, not something that God watched over, but the divine itself. His words accurately reflect Mayan attitudes toward the natural world that I have heard repeatedly expressed in myriad ways over the past several decades. The Mayan way is apparently not a path toward divinity as a distant goal. Instead, it weaves its way through a world where the divine is already immanently present.

The man's parting words to us as our hands touched included a warm wish that we wouldn't fall in the mud and another strong recommendation to visit Golondrinas, adding that it was just another hour away. After several more grueling hours on the trail and several more estimates that we would arrive in Golondrinas *"en una hora,"* we came to realize that an hour obviously did not mean the same thing among the Tenek Maya that it did on my inexpensive Japanese watch. As the sky began to darken slightly, we began to wonder if there really was such a place as Golondrinas. Scanning our rugged surroundings for a relatively flat place to set up our tent, we saw what appeared to be a large dark circle in the distant sky. As we hiked closer, we could see that the circle in the sky was actually rotating slowly and consisted of tens of thousands of tiny swallows, the famous golondrinas we had heard about from so many people on the trail.

After another half hour or so of walking, we found ourselves approaching a Tenek household living almost directly underneath the massive dark wheel of swarming birds. Several children rushed forward to greet us and motioned for us to follow them behind their thatched-roof home that had been simply fashioned from sticks and mud. As we walked across their rock-strewn backyard we came to what turned out to be the largest cave shaft in the world. The opening was a circle of exposed limestone perhaps 150 feet across. Although we kept well away from the edges of the chasm, we could see that the middle of the circle was a striking patch of deepest black. One of the young boys motioned to the sky and the rotating doughnut of birds above. As he did so, a group of perhaps twenty swallows broke from the circular formation and dove straight down toward the hole. All we could make out were dark streaks of downward movement as the birds hurtled by, wings tucked, producing a series of rapid swishes of sound. As we observed the scene in more detail, we could see that flocks of birds were continuing to join the group overhead from all directions and that they were all eventually headed to the thousands of nests that ringed the walls of the sinkhole. As the number of swallows began to diminish in the sky, flocks of bright green, loudly squawking parrots began to arrive and made their way into their own nests in the blackness below.

Growing Up in Nature

Curiosity forced me to my knees as I crawled forward toward the pit in order to get a better look. Nearing the edge, I felt currents of fear racing through my body that pushed me even closer to the rock, into a position lying flat on my belly. Dragging my prostrate body across the rock, I slowly pulled my head closer, peeked over the edge, and peered into the darkness. To my astonishment, there was no bottom in sight. With the rapid-fire sound of the diving swallows now just feet from my head, I could barely make out some of their minute movements in the limestone crevices along the descending walls. My eyes were beginning to adjust to the blackness when an unexpected impact struck lightly against the side of my body, sending a sudden jolt of fear shooting through my body. Looking quickly to the left, I saw the soles of the running bare feet of one of the Mayan boys scampering at full speed along the rim of the sinkhole. Once I recovered from the fright of the young boy's accidental kick, I realized that he and his brother were in the midst of some sort of game in which one was chasing the other around the edges of this massive pit, apparently oblivious to my precarious position and the potential danger of a fall. One misplaced footstep would result in certain death after a free fall that would be long enough to provide far too much time to appreciate such an unfortunate fate.

The last of the birds made their way into the sinkhole with the final traces of light in the western sky. We went with the boys to their house to ask permission to set up our tent at the edge of their cornfield. The father was not at home and their mother spoke little

Spanish; but we gathered that the family had always lived there and that they had no worries about the obvious dangers of the vast hole in the earth less than a minute from their doorstep. The kids who were old enough to get about on their own did so without supervision of any sort and without any apparent restrictions. They climbed in the highest branches of tall trees, handled their dad's finely honed machetes, and yes, even played tag on the rim of the gigantic sinkhole, with total abandon. Although this woman's apparent lack of concern may appear to be a lack of attentiveness to their safety, it exemplifies instead a pattern of deep and unspoken trust in their natural environment that I have witnessed on numerous occasions among the Maya.

As a Mayan *ahq'ih*[2] named Fabián Frías Santillán recently explained, "From the Mayan cosmovision, the human being is just another form of nature's design, another part in the infinite interweaving of forces in motion."[3] One consequence of that perspective is that Mayan parents living in rural areas generally allow their children to have unrestricted access to the physical world around them. The kids often go barefoot, never losing direct contact with the earth. Climbing in the trees, tending to their outdoor chores, splashing in rain puddles, and playing in the dirt, they learn nature's ways through physical experience, building a direct relationship with local ecosystems and other elements in their environment. In the process, they learn to identify and use dozens of plant species, come to understand the habits of both domestic and wild animals, and directly see their dependence on healthy natural systems for survival.

The underlying sacredness of the natural world sometimes manifests itself in the personification of animals and the description of inanimate objects and places as living entities. On one of my early visits to a Mayan settlement, I went with a friend with plans to set up our camp near a pleasant little stream. A large group of kids seemed to come out of nowhere to observe our activities. Since the vegetation near the water was quite dense, my friend pulled out his newly purchased machete and began to hack away at a sapling that was obstructing our proposed tent site. The children reacted immediately, trying to call attention to something. Our knowledge of their Tzeltal language did not go beyond a few phrases so we were confused as to what they were attempting to indicate to us. Finally, one of the older boys broke into the simple Spanish he was learning in school, *"El árbol está llorando"* ("The tree is crying"). The child's words stopped my friend's chopping and we managed to put up our tent in a slightly reduced area, far more appreciative of our surroundings.

Just as trees have feelings, other apparently nonsentient things and places can take on vital dimensions. An old Tenek shaman friend once invited me to a village ceremony that he was directing. He told me that the culmination of the ceremony was to be the passing on of an elaborately decorated wooden staff from the current village leader to the one for the coming year. His explanation of the stick itself was as follows:

> Roberto, the one thing that you need to remember about this ceremony is that this is no ordinary stick. It is alive. Do you understand? Do you see the green ribbons tied to its top? Can you feel its power? We pray to the four directions, especially when we need rain. But this staff is at the center. It is the source from which life flows. Remember, it is alive.

My friend's words point to one of the fundamental differences between Mayan ways and our own. Whereas we maintain a clear distinction between animate and inanimate elements of our world, Maya see all components of their experience as vital aspects of an integral living whole. In accord with the man we spoke with on the trail who said that everything was a living manifestation of "Father Sun," this village staff apparently was alive with spiritual and symbolic significance. Only years later, when studying Mayan culture formally at the University of Texas at Austin, did I learn that such staffs recall the green vertical axis at the center of ancient Mayan cosmology, the Yax Te'. They also recall the living staff held by the ancient rulers known as the deity K'awil, a word that I would translate as "instrument of rule."

The "living" Mayan landscape consists primarily of limestone in the northern and central lowlands that gives way in Guatemala to the uplifted mountains of the Cuchumatán range and, farther south, to a volcanic cordillera with still-smoldering craters. This geology has produced a land rich in sinkholes, caves, and prominent peaks that, for the nature-revering Maya, have been the focus of worship since ancient times. The openings into the earth are access portals into the inner realms of the divine, entryways to the hidden world of the ancestral spirits. Caves in the Mayan world often show evidence of very early ceremonial use such as glyphs on broken ceramic shards and written on the walls. Indications of ancient usage often exist alongside burning candles and evidence of ritual fires from contemporary worship. In one Mayan community, villagers ask a priest from a town several hours' walk away to come to their local cave to offer Mass on an annual basis. This massive cavern has a circular opening in the top measuring some ten feet in diameter that allows a shaft of daylight in to illuminate the space. The local shaman told me that he awoke to his calling in the cave when the light from above "entered" into him.

The Mayan focus on accessing the spirit through openings into the earth has its complement in their reverence for mountain peaks. Especially in highland Guatemala, the Maya view mountains as divine manifestations inhabited by special deities. These mountain deities often function as guardians for nearby communities. Sometimes a town will have four such guardians, one associated with each of the four cardinal directions. Worshippers often direct their words to the sacred peaks, asking for support or guidance. On rare occasion, the mountain spirit will respond through an interpreter. This happened when I attended a ceremony to determine if the oldest son in a family should risk a trip to the United States for work. After elaborate prayers and offerings, the woman conducting the ceremony began to speak in a strangely accented Mam and addressed the Mayan family's concerns regarding their son's travel plans. To my surprise, the mountain spirit then addressed a few words to me. It said that I was a very happy person and indicated that I was welcome in the living landscape lying in its massive shadow.

Much of the Mayan appreciation for the living universe is a simple result of a lifestyle that maintains ongoing contact between humans and their natural environment. Apart from sleeping and eating, rural Maya spend little time inside their rather modest houses. As soon as the sun begins to lighten the eastern horizon, Mayan farmers are outdoors on the way to work in their cornfields and they often do not return inside the house until dusk. Likewise, when not tending to the cooking fire, Mayan women spend almost all of their time working out-of-doors. Washing laundry often takes place at a public area with other women by a stream or another community water supply. Most homes have a small, covered porch area in front where they can weave, shell beans, and perform countless other chores that are part of the Mayan female domain. Children, of course, are outside virtually every waking moment, exploring the fields and trees around their home and playing with toys made from the sticks, stones, and earth at hand. Even when Maya spend time indoors after sunset, the separation from the surrounding natural environment is minimal. Mayan homes generally have no heat source beyond the cooking fire, and air-conditioning is nonexistent. Thus, most Maya are continuously aware of the outside air temperature, even when inside. Homes made of sticks, wooden slats, and thatch roofs let in the sounds of the wind, rain, thunder, birds, and other animals with minimal interference. It should come as no surprise then that Maya often develop a relatively high level of familiarity with nature's ways.

This total immersion in the natural world can have remarkable results. The late Mayan shaman José Guadalupe had developed extraordinary observational gifts. He had lived his entire life barefoot, directly feeling the earth beneath his feet continuously. He said that he had once tried shoes but they had made him feel uncomfortable. To some he seemed a bit crazy but I could not help but enjoy his affable company. Even when discussing the devastating deaths of family members said to be the work of an envious sorcerer in a neighboring village, he did so with an engaging lightheartedness of spirit. One day, he was determined to teach me a few of the names of the many birds living in the surrounding forest. He began by imitating each species' call and then pronouncing the word in his language. They called the local dove *kuku*. A small parrot species was a *q'ili*, another word that imitated the bird's call. He then came to a bird that I did not recognize by sound. When I asked for further explanation, he replied, "Roberto, don't you remember? Just three days ago one flew over us," motioning overhead to his right. I, of course, had no recollection of a solitary bird that flew by in a particular direction several days earlier. For a barefoot man immersed in the movements of nature since birth, however, such detailed observations were apparently the norm.

Practical experience reinforces this Mayan tendency toward a heightened appreciation of nature. When a person has to carry all the water the family needs each day, a deep respect for this life-sustaining liquid develops spontaneously. I experienced the depths of this respect one day when hiking to a distant village with a Mam elder who went to verify progress on a drinking-water project that he had helped get started. As is typical when Maya need to travel a great distance, we started out in the morning well before sunrise. The first hour or so passed under moonlight and in silence as we ascended at least two thousand feet. Once we were upon the ridge, the clear, early-morning sky gave us an unimpeded view of most of Guatemala's spectacular string of volcanoes, one sending up intermittent puffs of smoke and giving us a striking image of Earth as a breathing entity. After hours of unrelenting walking up and down steep grades, I saw a group of men in traditional clothing, with red, turbanlike head scarves, waiting for us around their newly built concrete water-distribution tank filled from a nearby spring.

As discussions took place among the assembly, another group of perhaps ten men emerged from around a corner on the trail and quickly approached us. My friend informed me in Spanish that the men had come to request a similar water project because they had located a good spring in a narrow valley several miles above their hamlet. As their homes were quite far away and my friend wanted to return home before dark, they said that we would need to run to the site of the spring. Within minutes, a dozen men were running down the trail with me and my aching legs bringing up the rear. Fortunately for me, much of the journey was downhill. As I began to take comfort in the descent, however, we suddenly veered off the trail and began a bushwhacking maneuver that took us scrambling down through some tall pines. The apparent craziness of our efforts, my fear of falling headlong into a tree, and the fact that nearly all the men were in their fifties and sixties kept me distracted from my growing exhaustion. When I began to wonder how much longer I could keep up with them, I saw that they had stopped down in a narrow spot not too far below me. We gathered around a crystal-clear pool of water perhaps four feet in diameter that flowed gently down the slope below. Once we had all arrived by the spring, without prompting, the men formed a circle around the tiny pool and began to pray. Even though my abilities in Mam are extremely limited, the one phrase that I kept hearing was *"Ch-honta tey, qman Dyos"* ("Thanks to you, our father God"). The intense reverence for this fountain of life-sustaining liquid was almost palpable. After we drank our fill of the cool waters, one man pulled out a measuring tape and we continued our descent to their settlement, calculating the number of lengths of pipe needed for the project. In the hamlet, the women gave my friend and me bouquets of fresh-picked flowers, presented us with ground corn in water to refresh us, and regaled us with beautiful words. Hours later, my legs literally trembling as we made our way back home, I felt humbled by my new understanding of the sacredness of water.

The Holy Maize

The Maya explicitly describe their literal oneness with the natural world. They say they are beings of corn. When I first heard of this belief, it struck me as a mere cultural curiosity. As I gained more experience living among Maya, however, it became apparent that this "belief" was not a mere mythological metaphor but a commonsensical description of Mayan physiology. The sacred grain is the principal ingredient in their diet. It is present at every meal in the form of tortillas, tamales, beverages, or roasted ears. My Mam friends in Guatemala view the consumption of tortillas as so integral to eating that they use the same word, *wabh*, both for "tortilla" and for "food" in general. Through the digestive process, the body converts the various forms of corn, along with the other foods eaten, into developing cells. The description of themselves as beings of corn is not merely a pretty way of talking about the importance of the grain in their lives. Maya literally are beings made from corn.

The *Popol Vuh* describes this practical reality in metaphorical terms when recounting the Mayan creator gods' attempts to fashion the first humans. Their first efforts using mud and sticks failed miserably since the new creatures were incapable of proper respect for their makers. Only through the intervention of nature in the form of four animals— a fox, a coyote, a parrot, and a crow—were the gods able to locate a suitable substance (corn) for molding the first humans. The site of the mythological fabrication of humanity—Paxil, the "Split Place"—is an actual location that lies in the Mam-speaking area of northwest Guatemala, and local lore confirms its place as the site of corn's origin. Interestingly, the mountain slopes in this area harbor the wild grain *teosinte*, a plant that seems closely linked to domestic corn. Paxil might quite literally be an origin site for what some Maya call "our Mother Corn."

Mayan scholar Barb MacLeod recently told me of a new discovery related to corn that she has made from her reading of hieroglyphic texts from the Naj Tunich caves in northern Guatemala.[4] According to her analysis, the ancient Maya living there made repeated references to *'ilah monpan,* "he attended [the ceremony of] the nurturing of the sprouts." This ceremony was apparently one that focused on nurturing babies, and the description of the infants as sprouts makes clear that they are the metaphoric equivalent to young stalks of corn. Maya tend to their sacred corn and their budding offspring with similar devotion.

Mayan farmers have patiently developed an amazing degree of genetic diversity in their favorite crop. In 1940, one investigator found 166 varieties of corn in the Cuchumatán highlands of Guatemala, not far from the traditional site of corn's purported origins.[5] Even a superficial peek into the rafters of a rural Mayan home will reveal an astonishing variety of kernel colors. I have even seen dried ears with a deep green hue. Reflecting the Mayan worldview that divides the surface of the Earth into four cardinal directions, the Maya see corn as having four basic colors: red, yellow, black, and white. Each color symbolically represents one of the directions. Red is the east. Yellow is the south. Black is the west. White is the north. Thus, corn represents the totality of the horizontal plane of the Earth. Not surprisingly, if we include the green cornstalk-like vertical axis at the center of the four directions, the symbolism of corn includes the entire cosmos. On numerous occasions, I have heard contemporary Maya extend this all-inclusive symbolism of corn to describe what they view as the planet's principal kinds of human beings: red, yellow, black, and white. Thus, corn implies both the entirety of nature and the humans who inhabit it as well. It comes as no surprise that some Mayan cultural activists refer to their homeland not as Guatemala but as Iximulew, the "land of corn."

The ubiquity of corn in Mayan life manifests in myriad ways. Not only is corn the main source of nourishment, growing it is the Maya's principal occupation. People consider corn production as an integral part of being Maya. In rural areas, even as Maya enter paid professional occupations as teachers or town officials and do not have time to prepare their own cornfields, they will pay someone else to grow corn on their behalf. In some communities, a stranger will sometimes inquire about the health of your corn before asking more personal questions. Maya use corn husks as food wrappers. They employ the dried tuft of "hair" from the ear as a stopper for their ceramic containers. After harvest, kite season begins in the highlands as Mayan boys assemble the lightweight stalks into simple flying contraptions. Mayan weavers use the water from making corn dough as a starching agent in preparing thread for weaving. They say that the corn gives needed strength to the cotton fibers so that they will not break during the weaving process. Corn covers the arable land surface in most rural areas of the Mayan world. It builds Mayan bodies as a food source and reinforces the fabric that covers them. It symbolizes the four directions, as well as the four branches of the human race, and even graces the windy sky in the form of kites after harvest.

Corn is the most sacred of all plants for the Maya and, as a result, even when an occasional plant pops up in an odd or inconvenient spot, people will invariably allow it to grow to fruition. A solitary cornstalk occasionally shoots up near the front door of a house or behind a rock on the trail, places where a random seed has fallen. The holiness of the plant even takes literary form in the *Popol Vuh* character named Hun Ahaw, "One Lord." Father of the famous mythical Hero Twins, he represents the Corn God. Also known as "First Father," the primordial ancestor of the Mayan people, Hun Ahaw's life is itself a metaphor for the corn cycle. In typical Mayan style, he has a dual nature and takes the form of twins named One Hunahpú and Seven Hunahpú. Like stalks of maturing corn, the twins eventually approach the realm of death, associated in the *Popol Vuh* with the black quadrant of the west. Upon their death, as Maya have done for centuries with their corn, the Lords of Death hang the head of One Hunahpú out to dry. His dried head, like a kernel of corn, remains fertile, and eventually engenders succeeding generations of Maya. The traditionalists of the Tz'utuhil Mayan community of Santiago Atitlán likewise emphasize the divine nature of corn by associating the figure of Jesus with the grain by drawing attention to the similarity between Jesus' flowing mane of hair and the tassel on an ear of corn.

The Mayan approach to corn is as practical as it is sublime. In the traditional corn garden, they grow the sacred grain in conjunction with at least two other plants, beans and squash. The growing stalks of corn provide an ideal natural trellis for the beans to climb, eliminating the need to manufacture any artificial structure. At the same time, the roots of the bean plants fix nitrogen into the soil and help nourish the corn. The squash plant spreads out vertically across the surface of the field with its broad leaves, protecting the soil from erosion during the rainy season.

The manner in which Maya prepare corn for eating reveals an ancestral and profound understanding of the grain. Apart from a small amount of corn that Maya consume fresh, they generally leave the grain to dry in the field by breaking the stalk so that the ears lie protected from the rain by the down-turned leaves surrounding them. Before consuming the dried ears, Maya soak them in a lime solution, a fine, white powder derived from "cooking" limestone cut from the earth below them. This alkaline solution loosens the hard membrane that surrounds the grain, which the cook then rinses away, leaving swollen, hominy-like grains known as *nixtamal*. Mayan cooks then grind these grains on an ancient tool made from volcanic stone, allowing them to produce extremely fine dough that they can use in preparing tamales, tortillas, or *atole,* a simple and refreshing beverage made from corn and water. Apart from the practical benefit of producing better dough, this preparation process also enhances corn's nutritional quality. It improves the balance of amino acids and frees niacin in the grains that would otherwise not be available. Although few Maya are consciously aware of these benefits, this special process of corn preparation reflects an ancestral knowledge of corn that has been essential to their collective survival.

The Mayan relationship with corn recently found expression during a visit to our home in Florida by a dear Guatemalan friend. During our conversation it occurred to me that she might enjoy seeing a particularly beautiful ear of red corn that I had been given on a recent trip to the Mayan highlands, thinking she might enjoy seeing something pretty from home. I quickly ran up the stairs, fetched the sunset-colored corn, and then handed it to our dear friend. She impulsively lifted the red ear of corn to her mouth and gently kissed it. Her lips spontaneously broke into a prayer of gratitude for the sacred sustenance of the Mayan people as millions have done before her. Her reflexive act of reverence for this life-giving grain silently conveys the millennial Mayan understanding that they are indeed people made from corn.

Mayan expertise in corn parallels extensive cultural knowledge regarding a wide range of wild and domesticated plants. On several occasions while I was helping in the "cleaning" of cornfields, Mayan friends have mildly reprimanded me for mistakenly uprooting edible plants. In some cases, Maya have lived in the same place for more than a hundred generations and their practical knowledge of the region's flora and fauna is formidable. In these rural areas, Maya consume numerous wild plants that enrich their diet with a wide variety of vitamins and minerals. They also make use of a remarkable number of medicinal herbs. The Mayan herbalist I know best regularly uses more than thirty different plants with her patients. Although some of her knowledge of plant medicine is specific to her midwifery practice, the majority of the remedies she employs commonly appear in the households of most in her community.

Body Knowledge

By living in communion with nature over multiple generations, Maya have developed a deep understanding and appreciation of natural systems. They have applied this experiential knowledge of the world around them to their own bodies, creating an approach to health and healing not unlike that of traditional Chinese medicine. Yukatek Maya in Mexico and Belize even use their own system of acupuncture, using thorns from plants instead of needles. Within this conceptual framework, personal well-being depends upon creating and maintaining balance, both within one's own body and with one's surroundings. The idea that a person must maintain a balance of hot and cold is just one manifestation of the Mayan approach to personal well-being. For the Maya, all foods and herbs are inherently either cooling or heating in the body when consumed. For good health, Mayans seek to maintain a state of equilibrium through their diet. Similarly, people must take care not to expose themselves to excessively hot or cold environments or they run the risk of health problems.

On a recent trip to Guatemala I had a direct experience of the Mayan heat-cold paradigm in practice. As often is the case, protesters from several K'iche' Mayan villages had blocked the principal road from Guatemala City up into the highlands, and the bus I was riding on sat for hours in a line of vehicles many miles long. The villagers were protesting the government's recent approval of a free trade agreement with the United States and they had halted all traffic on the Pan-American Highway. Although the unscheduled stop gave me the opportunity to meet many interesting people, the delay also caused me to miss a connecting bus to my final destination. As a result, like others headed farther up into the mountains, I boarded a huge cargo truck and stood with everyone else in the back, hanging on desperately to the wooden sideboards as the truck rocked back and forth on the extremely rough dirt road. As we approached about ten thousand feet in elevation, the damp air became frigid. I bundled up as best I could like everyone else on board but I was still having a tough time keeping my core temperature up. The road flattened out onto a large plain, shrouded in dense fog. The silhouettes of massive maguey plants and a few craggy oaks occasionally appeared and then faded in the ghostly mists. Between the penetrating cold, the dreary scenery, a building dehydration headache, and the diesel fumes in my nostrils, the conditions were starting to get the better of me. Just as the first pangs of nausea appeared we began to descend into a massive valley on the other side of the *altiplano*. Almost miraculously, we emerged from the fog into a cloudless sky and a view that extended perhaps fifty miles to the horizon. I was ecstatic and climbed up upon the truck's spare tire so I could take in the full expanse of the amazing beauty in front of us. The sunshine on my face and the strikingly blue sky above provided the illusion of much warmer temperatures. I happily tossed my jacket down to the floor on top of my travel bag. Conversations in Mam picked up all around, mothers let their little babies peek out from their protective cocoons of multicolored clothing, and the scent of the cedar replaced that of diesel fuel. I felt like singing. After arriving at my destination some forty-five minutes later, I could not wait to get my feet on solid ground and settle my shaken body down from the rough ride. I thought a lazy walk in the verdant countryside outside of town would be the perfect remedy. Unfortunately, I was wrong. Coming to a tiny rivulet, I simply leaped across. As I landed on my other leg, I felt an ugly movement in my spine. Within seconds I found myself in excruciating pain. I still don't know how I made it back up the hill to my friends' house in that condition. But once I was home, I remained virtually motionless in bed for three solid days.

During my forced convalescence, a steady stream of acquaintances stopped by to check on me. With each person, I went through the entire sequence of circumstances that had led to my injury. In every single case, the person ignored my jump across the stream but said that my problem was a result of the cold entering my back on the truck ride. They explained that my back had probably heated up under all my clothes and with all the warm bodies in the back of the truck. Taking off my jacket exposed my "hot" body to the cold far too quickly and my *k'an* ("cramp") was the unfortunate result. Whereas all gave me this explanation, several people added that the problem was more severe because I had just come from a "hot" place like Florida and had gone too quickly to a "cold" place like where they lived up in the mountains. Treatment for my condition focused on heating the area with massage and the application of some sort of herbal liniment meant to stimulate the tissues. The most valuable part of the treatment came about inadvertently but was every bit as Mayan. My Mayan friends lovingly joked about my injury and made fun of my inability to do anything. Although it might seem cruel, the joking was done so lovingly that several people had me shaking in uncontrollable laughter. The spasms of laughter shook my back painfully, and when I moaned, the silliness of the situation made us all laugh even more, provoking still more moans. To my delight, when my visitors left, I noticed my back had loosened up considerably, an unintended and most welcome result of my Mayan friends' love of humor. Ever since this incident, I have paid far greater attention to the Mayan perspective on temperature's effects on the body, an understanding that has arisen from generations of observing and learning from nature's ways.

In the era of 2012, the lessons of the living Maya have become vitally important. Our collective lack of appreciation for nature's ways has led us to live in ways that in the long run compromise the quality of our lives and even perhaps our survival. By encouraging our children and ourselves to come into deeper appreciation of our integrity with the natural world, our understanding of the divine reflexively shifts as well. The divine is no longer just an imaginary figure we pray to for solace, nor is it consciousness divorced from physical reality. Instead, we can come to the direct realization that nature is the living manifestation of the divine itself and we find ourselves incapable of deliberately doing her harm. By actively pursuing a lifestyle like that of the living Maya that enlivens our physical body and integrates deliberate sensitivity to its subtle workings, we can create ways of being human more in harmony with natural systems and begin to heal the horrific damage we have already inflicted on our planet.

CHAPTER **6**

Remember the Elders and Ancestors

K'iche' Mayan spiritual guide Rigoberto Itzep Chanchavac in Momostenango.

Respect Earned Through Life Experience

Along with their respectful treatment of babies, the living Maya seem to reflexively extend their highest regard to those of advanced age. Maya assume that the eldest members of their communities are also the wisest, simply by virtue of their having successfully survived so many years in such challenging circumstances. As recently as a generation ago, when encountering an elder out on the trail, Mam Mayan youngsters would approach them reverentially and request their blessings. The children would stand respectfully in front of the old man or woman and say *"Q'antz tq'aba"* ("Give me your hand"), and then bow their head forward. The elder would respond by lovingly placing the back of his or her hand against the child's forehead. Mothers with newborns would do something similar, holding their little one out from their carrying shawl so that the elder could place his or her thumb on the baby's forehead in blessing.

When in Guatemala I frequently get a close-up view of how the living Maya perceive their elders each time I get to spend the day with a dear Mayan friend, Martín, who has been one of the most positive influences in my life. He is one of the most highly regarded people in the entire county-size area. There is an almost continual flow of townspeople stopping by my friend's home for advice, reminding me of the profound esteem that some senior members of the community enjoy. Young men stop by for his thoughts on a troubled marriage or on urgent community issues. Women might inquire about how to start a family business or ask to speak with his kindhearted spouse who, as the female counterpart of this couple, has long served as a local midwife. Together they form the most inspirational couple I have ever met, a comment that I know, if they ever heard it, would have them laughing out of genuine humility. Children come by, standing politely "at attention," and ask Martín or his wife politely to take fruit from their large organic orchard, and old men stop simply to recall memories from decades past. His fellow townspeople so value my friend's suggestions and ideas that a simple walk for an errand on the other side of town can take several times longer than it should due to the number of individuals wishing to interact with him. On occasion, as we've approached town from a distant settlement, he has even advised me to follow him through some back trails and alleyways so he can temporarily avoid conversations and get home for a meal with his wife.

Martín is a teacher whose sole pedagogical technique is setting a good example. I have met hundreds of his family, friends, and acquaintances and they unanimously respect him and have fond memories of working with him. That's because he has worked hard his entire life and continues to do so well after our typical retirement age. As a young man, he worked carrying carefully lashed stacks of eggs on his back using the traditional Mayan headstrap from his remote valley community up over a ten-thousand-foot, chilly plateau and then down several thousand feet into the next valley. The trip now takes two hours in a motor vehicle. The image of Martín carrying nearly his own body weight in eggs for many hours at high elevations and up and down extraordinarily steep inclines is suggestive of the way he has lived his entire life. For decades this exemplary elder has been at the forefront of efforts to reforest the massive valley he calls home. Not long ago, I gained access to a photo of the valley from the mid-1950s and was able to compare the image with a photo I had taken from precisely the same spot. To my delight, the valley appeared much more heavily forested in my photo, and I have come to realize that much of the credit for improving the health of the environment in this valley goes to Martín's sustained efforts. His people admire and respect Martín for his unrelenting work improving their community, his modest lifestyle, measured words, and transparently humble demeanor.

Shortly after the Zapatista rebellion broke out in Chiapas in 1994, I attended a talk in Austin, Texas, by representatives of the Mayan rebels. The meeting was being sponsored by local Quakers and the large hall was packed to overflowing with interested university students and members of the local community. After a long wait, I could see three Tzotzil Maya, two women and a man, all perhaps in their thirties, climb to the stage and take their seats. After a few preliminary words, the three Mayan guests were introduced to the crowd with a round of warm applause. As the applause began to fade, the man hesitatingly approached the microphone, his eyes downcast toward the seats in front of him. The translator motioned him forward, encouraging him to speak ... but nothing came. He stood there in silence, seemingly confused as to what he was to do or say. Those in the room began feeling uncomfortable for the poor man, sensing that he was not used to public speaking. Finally, after at least a full minute, the man muttered in Spanish that he "had not realized that there would be elders this evening." Motioning toward the front row of the assembly, he bowed forward slightly, drawing my attention to a group of white-haired seniors. He was referring to *our* elders and assumed the genuinely humble attitude of any young Mayan man when faced with those he assumed to be embodiments of experientially acquired wisdom. In his own world in the highlands of Chiapas, it would be the elders who speak and he would respectfully listen. What had at first seemed to me to be discomfort with public speaking was instead a deeply engrained respect for those considered to be most knowledgeable.

Some years ago, I traveled with my young son and a dear friend to renew acquaintanceships among the Tenek Maya of northeastern Mexico. Although I had walked to many hamlets in the eastern flanks of the Sierra Madre Oriental on several prior occasions, there was one particular community in the area that I had never visited and had been curious about for years. After perhaps two hours hiking on the trail through lush vegetation, we heard a male voice yell down to us from somewhere in the dense green above our path. Although we could not see anyone or understand what had been said, we stopped our walking to be sure there was not someone who needed help. After a few minutes, an older man with an especially sweet face climbed out of the greenery next to us and addressed us in his own language. I apologized for speaking only Spanish, and the man immediately shifted into our common second tongue. He insisted that we come with him a bit farther up the hill in order to meet his father. As we ascended the steep trail, our host said, with genuine enthusiasm that we were the first outsiders that he had ever seen there, and I now assumed he wanted to "show us off" to the rest of his family, his dad in particular. When we eventually arrived, now covered with sweat, at the family compound, the man whisked us past assorted family members and took us directly into the smallest structure there. In the middle of the room, sitting on a tiny bench, was a slight, very elderly man with a huge smile whom we learned was our host's father. He sat on the bench in a massive pile of corn kernels of various colors. I couldn't help but notice his broad feet and toes spread wide from never wearing shoes as they rested atop the mound of sacred grain. The only other thing in the room was a makeshift table that had been converted into an altar festooned with fresh white flowers. With the elder's son acting as translator, I was told that the old man's age was unknown but that we know that he had escaped to this remote place when, during the Mexican Revolution (1910–20), armed groups (he didn't really know whose side they were on) came looking to force young Tenek into their ranks. As this extraordinary elder spoke, I could sense the son's immense pride and his delight in having introduced us. As the conversation continued, we were served delicious tortillas fresh off the griddle, lightly sprinkled with dried hot peppers that were as tasty as any I've ever had. Even though the family seemed curious about us, I soon became aware that no one was particularly excited by the fact that we were there. Instead, what they saw as so special about our encounter was that *we* had been so amazingly fortunate to meet the family's most senior member. I had completely misunderstood the source for everyone's happiness. They were thrilled by *our* good luck on meeting this beloved, and still working, great-grandfather.

The high regard for elders can even manifest itself in ways that might strike us as extreme. I was once with my wife in a small town that was celebrating the feast day of St. Martín, its patron saint. After visiting the crowded church and paying our respects to the saint's image, we slowly made our way through the dirt streets, which were jammed with religious celebrants. At one point, to my horror, I saw an elderly man, apparently unconscious from intense drinking, lying face down in the dirt in front of me. Rather than stepping around or over him as all the others were, I felt inclined to help the man and at least move his body out of harm's way. Rather than involve my wife in hauling the man's limp body, I asked a middle-aged man nearby to help carry the elder to the side of the earthen road. The man looked at me rather sternly and began to scold me, quite annoyed that I would be so bold. "This man has lived many years. He is a *tih xhal,* an 'ancient person.' If he wants to rest in the road, that is his choice. Leave him alone." This extreme respect for what seems to be an elder's poor choice manifests the high regard afforded all senior members of their community.

On one occasion, we were fortunate to bring a Mayan family to our university for a series of cultural activities. Although I wanted to have my students learn as much as possible about Mayan ways, I also wanted my visitors to learn about North American society. I had arranged for the family to visit a local retirement center, one of the nicest in our area, in order to give a little presentation on Mayan culture. The place was quite luxurious and included everything from a swimming pool to a formal dining room. Apparently, I had not adequately explained where we were going to our Mayan guests. As the seniors slowly made their way into the meeting room and took their seats, I noticed a sadness come over the face of the Mayan woman sitting next to me. Within seconds, she was weeping uncontrollably. Her husband tried to come to her rescue by saying that seeing all the elders together had reminded his wife of her father, who had died when she was young. Once she calmed down, the talk went wonderfully. At the event's conclusion, the seniors all came forward to hug their guests. Once out the door on our way home, the Mayan woman explained her teary outburst. "Where are their families?" she asked. "How can they be left here away from their loved ones? The *tij* ['ancient ones'] are our precious ones, our jewels." I did my best to explain to her the concept of retirement and our tendency for extended families to live apart from one another, but my words seemed to fall on deaf ears. The Mayan respect for their elders runs so deep that the concept of having them live outside the family home is virtually unthinkable.

The only other time this Mayan woman was upset during her visit in the United States was on a similar tour to a preschool program. When she saw the dozens of beautiful little ones in their well-maintained school, to my surprise she broke into tears, asking, "Where are their mothers?" When I explained that they had to work in order to help support their families, she did not seem convinced that this was a sensible approach. This high regard for both babies and the elderly is the norm among the Maya. In some cases, Maya make the tie between their communities' youngest and oldest members quite explicit. In the Mam language, for example, the word for "grandfather," *chman*, is identical to the word for "grandchild." The babies are what many Maya call the "replacements" for the elders, an idea that suggests a uniquely Mayan form of reincarnation. Before passing on into the ancestral realm, Mayan elders hope to see their own faces mirrored by those of their grandchildren, ensuring the continuity of their own bloodline and of their people. Once the elders die, Maya believe that they continue to counsel and support their descendants from beyond the grave.

Death Among the Maya

Maya share a far more keen awareness of nature's cycle of death and rebirth that we do, since it is a drama that unfolds in front of their eyes daily and that helps them see human death within this vast context. Just as children typically witness or participate in most other aspects of community life, Maya regularly participate in funerals from an early age. I frequently ask university students in my own classes how many dead human bodies they have seen in their lives. There are many who have never even seen one, but most answer that they have seen one or two of their grandparents' bodies and occasionally perhaps that of a parent or sibling laid out in funeral parlors. If I were to ask the same question to young Mayan adults in a rural community, the numbers would often reach into the dozens. Not only have they seen the dead of their own families, but the dead of most of the families they know and even many of those in numerous other families in the area.

Maya typically open their doors to public wakes with ritual wailing and elaborate feasts, often followed by a musical procession accompanying the body to the graveyard. In one Mayan town I am familiar with, the cemetery is the site of what is by far the most important festival of the year. Families spend several days and nights at the graves of their beloved ancestors, conversing with the ancient spirits and making ritual offerings of food and drink. They see human death as part of a continuous and natural process rather than as a tragic fate.

Maya make no attempt to sugarcoat death, but instead, due to their traditional lifestyle that brings them into an ongoing relationship with nature's cycles, they view it within a vast, but truly mundane, context. This of course does not lessen the sorrow Maya experience over the deaths of loved ones; I know many Maya still weeping over the violent deaths of family members in the Guatemalan civil war that occurred decades ago. However, by collectively seeing death in the context of nature, Maya are not inclined toward self-pity nor do they tend to become obsessed with blaming others or circumstances for a loved one's death. They know through a lifetime of direct and unfiltered observation that all humans, including themselves, will inevitably die and it is merely a question of time.

In one of my first encounters with the Mayan understanding of death, I was returning from a long hike to a neighboring town when I noticed a crowd gathered in the courtyard of a family compound located just off the trail I was using. Not wanting to be too intrusive, I kept my attention straight ahead on the path and thought I might be able to walk by unnoticed. However, just as I passed the front entry into the group of adobe structures, an older man called out to me, *"Ti ma txi, tat? Kixta tzalu"* ("Where are you going, sir? Come over here"). I walked back to greet him, we touched hands ever so lightly, and he motioned for me to follow. I was ushered into a one-room home that seemed packed with people. Once my eyes more fully adjusted to the candlelight inside, I could see that the visitors were focused toward the center of the space, where an open coffin sat upon some sort of platform or table. The man who had invited me in pointed to what I would later find out was his friend's body, and proclaimed simply, *"Tx'otx'"* ("He is earth"). For Maya, who in rural areas are virtually all farmers, we humans are ultimately just like any other animal, or plant for that matter, that, when its allotted time has expired, decays once again into the soil, enriching the earth for the next season of growth.

As mentioned, the vast context of nature does little to temper the devastating personal experience after the loss of a loved one but the Mayan approach to how to integrate the death is quite different from our own. Our own society typically attempts to minimize death's impact by keeping it at as much distance as possible. Mortuary practices make the dead body look as lifelike as possible. Often we keep the casket closed to minimize the discomfort of funeral participants. Maya, on the contrary, seem to deliberately immerse themselves in the pain of separation in order to more fully and thoroughly experience their loss. The body of the deceased usually lies on a table or bed in the middle of the small home for all to see. Throughout the day and early evening, guests arrive, bearing contributions of food and liquor. The liquor flows freely, allowing for an uninhibited expression of sorrow. Often, Mayan women further heighten the atmosphere of sadness with their ritualized wailing. The Mayan sense of shared awareness further reinforces the already overwhelmingly charged ambience.

During one wake I attended, in the midst of eating and drinking, a heart-wrenching scream startled me from a conversation with an old friend. In the doorway of the adobe home, the twentysomething son of the man who had just died stood with his arms spread wide. He let out another horrific scream at the top of his lungs and collapsed face down on the dirt in front of the body, racked with uncontrollable sobbing. As some of the assembled neighbors reached to help the young man, his uncle groaned loudly and fell down on the patio, lying next to his nephew, embracing him with his own shaking body. With a group of wailing women intensifying the atmosphere of grief with their droning cries, the scene took on a depth of emotional outpouring that was completely new to me. Although one could argue that the heavy consumption of alcohol in this setting is unhealthy, it may also be that the emotional release facilitates the grieving process and ultimately speeds the recovery of the deceased's loved ones.

Living with the Ancestors

There are contemporary Maya who continue the tradition of remembering those who have preceded them as they attempt to live in accord with the wisdom of ancestral experience. Many Mayan midwives say that the ancestral connection is the underlying basis of their professional lives and that their skills with birthing come directly to them from visiting spirit beings from ancient days, usually in their dreams. One midwife friend told me of a dream she had as a young woman in which a group of ancestral elders presented themselves to her with a book. The dream repeated itself with increasing regularity as she simultaneously developed a series of severe illnesses that culminated in a period of intense headaches. Fearing that she might not survive, she went for a consultation with a neighborhood *chmanbah*,[1] the local shaman. He told her that the suffering resulted from her not accepting the ancestral book offered by the spirit beings, a volume that symbolized the knowledge needed to practice the profession chosen for her by the ancient ones. In a subsequent dream she held the ancestors' book in her hands, and in her waking state she soon felt relieved of her symptoms. Still childless and in her teens, she remained uncertain about what was happening to her and, in particular, she wondered how she would perform her work without sufficient training. She returned to her *chmanbah* with her concerns and he told her to return home. He said she already had received the *cargo* from the *principales* and that her first patient was waiting for her. When she arrived back at her house, nobody new was at home and she nearly started to get angry with the old shaman. Before she could, however, a young mother came to her, carrying an infant baby who seemed dangerously weak. Upon laying eyes on the little one, the prospective midwife reflexively knew which plant to seek out and she prepared an infusion that eventually healed the baby. From the very first moment of her practice she felt guided by a spontaneous curative knowledge that she firmly believes came to her as a gift in a dream vision of her ancient ancestors. Like Lady K'abal Xok, the queen of Classic Period Yaxchilan, this modern woman depends on an inner connection with those in the spirit realm to illuminate her days among the living with wisdom and direction from generations past.

For many contemporary Maya, there are visual reminders of this realm of the dead close at hand in the form of ancient ruins once lived in by their predecessors and cemeteries of more recent origin. Almost every Mayan community has ready access to limestone structures used by their people for hundreds, if not thousands, of years. Not long ago, a young Mayan mother was walking up through the ruins near the center of her town, known locally as Qmantxun, literally, "the limestone of our fathers." She felt a tiny tug on her *amh*, the immense, circular indigo blue cloth that serves as the standard skirt for women in her town. As they left the ruins site, her toddler son was signaling for her attention but she was more intent on encouraging him to walk up the hill. When he persisted, she looked down to see him hold out a bright green jade bead with a hole neatly drilled through the middle. The bead was no doubt a burial piece that had washed out from the rubble of one of the temple mounds by the winter rains. He and all in his family felt delighted by the find. I wondered at what it must be like to be a young Mayan boy and find something within minutes of your home likely made a thousand years earlier by a distant relative. Such events implant a sense of belonging, both to a place and to an ancestral heritage, that is now difficult for most of us to imagine.

My sole personal experience related to the Mayan ancestral realm was momentary and it occurred in an exquisitely simple dream, but it was so remarkable and transformative that it has convinced me of the ancestral realm's potential existence, even if I am at a loss to adequately explain it. Although I am disinclined to put too much stock in the nocturnal revelations of my dreamworld, this particular dream left me so profoundly awestruck by its power that it seemed significantly more "real" than my everyday waking reality. My dream vision was of an ancient-looking woman in traditional clothing who was kneeling on a reed mat absorbed in her weaving. The dream itself lasted no more than twenty seconds, no words were spoken, no conceptual information was involved, and no events took place. The ancestral woman focused completely on her backstrap loom and paid me no attention at all. While the scene itself was static apart from the ancient one's rhythmic weaving movements with her loom, my own being was immobilized with overwhelming sensation. I felt as if a powerful electric charge was vibrating throughout my body, shaking me to my core. More significantly, I simultaneously experienced such intense gratitude, awe, and compassion that I became virtually blinded by uncontrollable tears, making it difficult to see the source of this radical shift into more deeply informed awareness. In India, to be in the presence of beings capable of catalyzing such awakening energy is called having *darshan* with a saint. For the Maya, contact with such powerful spirits would likely be perceived as having a family connection. It seems possible that living Maya not only pass down states of consciousness from one generation to the next through the enriched interactions within the home, but they may also do so with ancestral beings inspiring the living Maya through the medium of dreams using unseen psychic mechanisms lying outside of our own culture's realm of possibilities.

I have often wondered how to explain the collectively experienced heightened state of awareness that June and I first encountered among Maya living in the remote Ch'ol communities of Chiapas more than thirty years ago. For the two of us, it required daily ingestion of dozens of psilocybin-bearing mushrooms over a period of two weeks before our beings opened into this powerfully enhanced consciousness. But the Ch'ol people we were meeting at that time had, to our knowledge, not deliberately done anything to induce this state, nor did they even seem curious about the "magic" mushrooms, even though they knew of their effects. To my surprise, through processes I still do not comprehend, these people were already established naturally in the radically expanded awareness that the mushrooms had produced in June and me without their actually having taken any of them.

Many factors may have contributed to this rather astonishing phenomenon. Recall that Maya deliberately encourage development of a complex web of connections to nature formed through a lifetime of unfettered daily interactions with local ecosystems. For instance, these particular people were, at that time, living barefoot nearly all of the time, hours from the nearest road and without access to electricity. At their suggestion, June and I stopped wearing shoes as well. Even though we kept this up for only about six months due to the intense social pressures against bare feet at home in the United States, it was still enough time to directly experience the notable sense of well-being that can come from literally being connected to the earth without the insulating effects of rubber soles. I also suspect that the lack of ambient chatter contributed to these people's capacity for heightened awareness. Without the almost continuous "hum" of motors, recorded music, television, and radio chatter that has become normalized in the developed world, they lived in a silence interrupted only by birdsongs, wind rustling through the trees, and the sounds of water in the form of rain or streams flowing over the sculpted limestone.

The potential inner tranquillity produced by this natural environment, combined with the powerful psychological bonds between humans established at birth and broadened to include the extended family and community, might be sufficient to make possible the enhanced awareness that was so apparent among these villagers. However, I think it's possible that ties to their Mayan ancestors may also inform their consciousness. Since traditional Maya place such high value on the significance of their dreams, and simultaneously maintain profound reverence for their ancestors, it may be that their lives are enriched through dream encounters with the ancient ones, just as my own life has been. It also may be possible that their distant ancestors' ingestion of awareness-enhancing substances may have had genetic effects that can spontaneously unfold in future generations of descendants, especially those immersed in traditional lifestyles that facilitate development of enriched consciousness.

In this era of 2012, living Maya can provide a model for shifting into a renewed relationship with our past. Like Maya, we have our own elders we can learn from. Unfortunately, perhaps more than people in any prior generation, our elders here in the United States came of age during a time of our greatest societal delusion. This is the group that journalist Tom Brokaw called "the greatest generation" for its ability to endure the hardships of the Great Depression and for the industriousness it showed re-creating the United States as a world power. From my own perspective, however, it was this same genera-tion that, without realizing it was doing so, pulled our society furthest away from the traditional ways of the living Maya. Some members of this deluded generation made every effort to divorce themselves from the natural world, seeing themselves as those destined to subdue and control it. They shifted our birth paradigm toward what is in many ways an industrial model, built for expediency and profits. In nearly every dimension of our lives, machines were built to make our lives easier and more comfortable, neglecting to realize that each step in this direction can also lead to unforeseen diminishment of the quality of our life experience. They created churches based on a largely super-ficial relationship to spirit, relying increasingly on conceptually based approaches and the formation of communities lacking much soul. Perhaps because of their material privations during the Great Depres-sion, they instilled in our society a collective desire for the acquisition of material goods that has infected every generation since and has now spread to cultures around the globe. Still, millions of souls in this most deluded generation managed to avoid the popular mainstream of their times and have lived truly inspiring lives that now serve as valuable models and sources of wisdom. Although they might not be as easy to find as among contemporary Maya, our own wise elders do indeed exist and have much to offer us if we make the effort to seek their company.

Another opportunity afforded by following Mayan ways is to integrate a greater awareness of death's reality into our daily experience. Rather than avoiding the topic as is our practice, we could, like living Maya, deliberately recall that death comes for all of us, that our time here among the living is short and precious. To the extent that we can genuinely embrace the reality of our impending deaths, we spontaneously live more earnestly, take ourselves less seriously, and deliberately seek out genuinely transformative and uplifting spiritual experiences.

CHAPTER 7

Experience the Spirit

*K'iche' Mayan spiritual guide Rigoberto Itzep Chanchavac
invoking spirits from the four directions.*

The Divine Is Omnipresent

I once had the opportunity to speak with Johannes Wilbert when
he came to visit a class I was taking with the late Mayanist Linda
Schele. Dr. Wilbert is an ethnographer with more than a half century
of experience with the Warao people of the Orinoco River delta in
Venezuela and undoubtedly one of the Westerners most familiar with
the Native American world. He unintentionally impressed me with a
preliminary statement that he was only now beginning to grasp more

fully the extent of his own ignorance concerning Warao cosmology. Taking the rare chance to speak with such a genuinely knowledgeable person, I asked what he thought was the most fundamental difference between indigenous peoples in the Americas and mainstream Western culture. He did not hesitate for a second and immediately mentioned the realm of spirituality. In Wilbert's terminology, the Western approach to spirituality is what he called "transcendent"—that is, that the divine is an entity, process, or force above and beyond mere mortals. For indigenous Americans, on the contrary, the spirit is "immanent," immediately unfolding as one's direct experience. Wilbert's description of native spirituality applies full force to the Mayan world. Among living Maya, human beings' relationship with the divine is primarily a matter of awareness and direct experience rather than one based on mere belief and conceptual understanding. For Maya still living within a traditional framework, there exists a sense of living within divinity rather than believing in a distant Creator who keeps watch and listens to our prayers from on high, even though these approaches are not mutually exclusive.

The Mayan approach to spirituality reveals itself in the words of the first Mayan novelist, Gaspar González, particularly in his first book, *A Mayan Life*. Early in the novel, the protagonist's family deliberately helps bring the young Lwin into direct relationship with the divine over a three-day period of ritual and contemplation. The young boy's father explains to him, "It's the Spirit that lives in every place and in every moment." Its "presence floods everything that exists, fills the earth day and night, the heights and the depths, the right and the left, behind and before. For that reason, our crosses represent the totality of the universe, the four corners sustained by the presence of God."[1] On the last day of the boy's initiation experience, his grandfather takes him up to a sacred mountain peak where "Lwin was inundated with a sense of divine grandeur, and he lost track of time watching the sky … He was truly happy."[2] The words recall my own experience with June on a Mayan hilltop as a young man and recall Dr. Wilbert's description of an indigenous divinity that is ever ready to reveal itself.

A wise older woman once gave me a clear reminder of the immediacy and intimacy of Mayan spirituality. I arrived in her community for the first time in the late morning in order to practice my language skills. I could not see a single soul in the tiny village so I began to wander down toward what I thought might be a stream. As I passed by a low-lying adobe structure, a small group of women began to emerge. Reluctant to make any of them fearful inadvertently, I refrained from approaching them and instead called out a friendly greeting in their language. Almost immediately, the woman who seemed to be the oldest in the group responded and walked in my direction. Thinking incorrectly that I could speak her language, she made some initial inquiries that were far beyond my meager abilities to comprehend. Noticing my bewilderment, she tentatively tried out a few simple phrases in Spanish and when she heard that I could understand, we began a rather clumsy conversation in a mixture of Spanish and her own language.

I soon realized that this was a very substantial person with a strong presence and vast life experience. As is my habit when meeting such people, I tried to inquire about her spiritual life. After some initial confusion and hesitation, she seemed to grasp my question and began to speak with renewed vigor. I lost track of what she was trying to say but saw that she was making sweeping gestures toward the sky and then making a similar movement toward the earth. Since many of her words were in her own tongue, I had no clear idea what she was trying to tell me. Falling back on my background as a lapsed Catholic, I asked her if perhaps she was referring to the concepts of heaven and hell. To my surprise, the look on her face turned to one that seemed to be a mixture of pity and dismay. Focusing intently on her Spanish pronunciation, she said the equivalent of the following: "No, young man. This is not about heaven and hell. Above us is our Father, the sun. Below us is our holy Mother who feeds us." In a remorseful tone, she added, "We scratch her face." For this Mayan woman, God was not a fanciful entity in her imagination but an intimately familiar and life-giving sun that she could see directly above us and that warmed our skin. It was not a divine being meting out punishment for us in the fiery bowels of the Earth, but a literally nourishing maternal presence directly under her bare feet. The "scratches" that we inflict upon Mother Earth's face are the furrows the Maya cut into her with their hand tools using ancient agricultural practices. The apparent sense of regret this woman felt regarding her people's farming arises naturally from her sense of familial connection with an ultimately benevolent and immediately present living cosmos.

While contemporary Maya accept a variety of religious belief systems, this diversity exists in the context of spiritual immediacy as described by Wilbert. In every external expression of Mayan spirituality I have witnessed, the depth of experience of the participants and the intensity of their activities far exceed what exists in our own traditions. Historically, Maya would draw blood from their own bodies using obsidian blades and stingray spines as a sacrificial offering to the divine in hope of receiving guidance from their divine ancestral spirits. Diego de Landa, a Catholic bishop in the Yucatán during the colonial period, described numerous kinds of highly intense ritual sacrifice, including making cuts around their ears and piercing their cheeks and lips. The Yukatek Maya even continued the Classic Period practice of drawing blood from the male member. According to Robert Bruce, the traditional Lacandon Maya of Najá in Mexico performed an incense burner renewal ceremony that lasted an almost incredible two months. He reported that he and the other participants stayed in the so-called "god house for nearly the entire period, even sleeping there in the cramped confines, enduring the cold nights with great physical discomfort."[3] Modern Maya who follow indigenous spiritual traditions often walk great distances and endure harsh climatic conditions in order to worship and make offerings at outdoor shrine sites in caves or on sacred mountains. Often, in preparation for such worship, spiritual practitioners will forgo sexual activity for an extended period and thereby increase their inner strength and the intensity of their efforts. Some Maya even fast before performing such ceremonies—once again, with the purpose of intensifying the experience by increasing their sensitivity. The vast majority of Maya now practice some variant of Christianity, but even here, their passionate practice of the faith reveals a commitment less dependent on conceptual belief than experiential awareness. I have witnessed evangelical services that continue around the clock for three days, with participants taking only rare breaks before returning to their prayers and song. Even the Catholic Mass I grew up with can become, in the Mayan context, a marathon event lasting hours, with small children coming and going for bathroom breaks and snacks.

People of the Holy Cross

I recently witnessed another expression of the depths of Mayan devotion to the spirit in one of the villages of the Macewal Maya, the so-called People of the Cross who live in the eastern Yucatán Peninsula. The Macewal live in relatively isolated communities not far from the modern tourist centers that have sprung up along the Caribbean coast. Their history must surely be one of the most interesting in the Western Hemisphere.

Like nearly all Mayan peoples, those living in the Yucatán Peninsula have been victims of severe racism and discrimination since the arrival of the first Europeans in the early 1500s. By the middle of the nineteenth century, Mexico had become an independent nation and the elite of Yucatán were beginning to grow two new cash crops, sugar and henequen. These new plantation industries required a large workforce and before long, large numbers of Maya found themselves working as debt peons. As dissatisfaction and tensions rose among the Maya, small skirmishes and mutual massacres between Mexicans and Maya finally erupted into full-scale warfare in 1847. With the ruling whites weakened by factional politics, the rebellion quickly gained adherents, including even disaffected non-Maya, and achieved numerous initial victories. Thousands of Maya, freed from the bonds of servitude, ravaged white settlements, killing everyone in their path. By May 1848, government forces were staggering in retreat toward Mérida and their other strongholds, their morale nearly broken by the Mayan onslaught. The 140,000 non-Maya under siege waited for what seemed to be certain annihilation. Surprisingly, however, when scouting parties went out to assess the Mayan forces, there were none to be found. The Maya surrounding the remaining whites had become short on supplies awaiting their final assault. And then, as food rations dwindled, the Mayan soldiers had spotted a particular species of winged ant that marked the beginning of the season for planting corn. Knowing that their families' survival depended on the sacred grain, they simply had left the battlefield and returned home to their cornfields. The relieved whites regrouped with an abundant influx of arms and food. They then launched a highly successful counterattack with the help of nearly a thousand U.S. mercenary soldiers that routed the Mayan rebels, forcing them into the protective forests of the eastern Yucatán. The war produced severe loss of life for both Maya and whites, with the overall population of the peninsula dropping 40 percent between 1848 and 1850.[4]

The Mayan rebels, reeling from their losses, found an unlikely savior in the form of a "speaking" cross. A small band of Maya purportedly found the cross at a place called Lom Ha, in a naturally occurring sinkhole. Such openings into the earth, of course, symbolically provide access to the hidden realm of the divine. Further reinforcing the sacred context, a large ceiba tree, the Mayan representation of the cosmic axis at the center of the world, grew from the cave's mouth. A man named Juan Puc felt convinced that the cross was speaking to him, just as other Mayan oracle figures had in pre-Columbian times at sites such as Cozumel. As the sacred cross's spokesperson, Juan began to make proclamations, stating that the followers of the cross would defeat the whites, even promising the Mayan militia protection from enemy bullets. Even though the first attack by the Macewal was repelled with heavy Mayan losses, the symbol of Mayan spirituality quickly gained new converts. In an attempt to short-circuit the rebellion, white forces attacked the Macewal capital at Noh Cah Santa Cruz Balam Nah ("Great Town of the Holy Cross Jaguar House") and destroyed the cross but they found it impossible to control the region.

Perhaps as many as 50 percent of the government forces in the field died in action.[5]

Mayan losses on the battlefield were also severe, but the spiritual symbolism of the cross, now nourished with the blood of the war dead, was irresistible to a culture that prioritized the realm of the spirit over the mundane. The People of the Cross launched repeated attacks on government forces, several times retaking their sacred center and several other key towns, eventually carving out an area where they could grow the sacred corn and honor their holy cross without interference. Government attempts to assault the Mayan strongholds failed miserably. In one costly expedition against the Macewal, all but 500 of more than 2,800 government soldiers died. The Macewal, under the direction of the cross's spokesman at the time, had the custom of executing virtually all white prisoners, further escalating the intensity of the conflict. Decades of warfare, internecine conflict, and excessive work demands also took a tragic toll on the Macewal, whose numbers stood at perhaps only six thousand people by the turn of the century. Mexican government forces captured the rebel capital permanently in 1901 before a wave of smallpox further decimated the Macewal population. Even so, the rebel Maya would not submit. By 1929, the Macewal could no longer maintain their presence at their "capital" at Noh Cah Santa Cruz Balam Nah, and the surviving 700 people took their cross to its final home in a tiny village still deeper in the hinterland.

Several years ago, my wife and I accompanied a few university students for a visit in this shrine site of the holy cross, where I hoped to be able to pay our respects. As we rolled into town past a small cross that marked the edges of this sacred setting, I began to feel apprehensive. I had read for years that outsiders to this community were not welcome. The reputation made sense given their brutal interactions with the outside world. As a remnant of its violent history, the Macewal communities maintained a quasi-military structure to protect the holy cross from the so-called tz'ulo'ob, the non-Mayan enemies of their people. Several local villages took turns providing guards on a weekly basis, with the men staying in permanent barracks that each community maintained at the shrine site.

Instead of the hostile reception that I feared, however, upon arriving at the village center, laughing teenagers on bicycles surrounded us with a crowd of their smiling smaller siblings in tow. This was hardly the belligerent attitude I had expected. Our unofficial guides walked us directly to the heart of the shrine site's ceremonial center, the community house along with the temple known as the Balam Na, or House of the Jaguar. Both structures were quite large by the standards of typical Mayan homes but shared the traditional thatched palm roofing found on every house in the village. Since no adults seemed to be in the vicinity, the youngsters suggested that we visit the town's principal natural feature, a moderate-size sinkhole only a few minutes away. After exploring the underground chambers for a few minutes, we returned to the village center to find that several men had returned. Each neighboring village sent a contingent of guards to protect the shrine site on alternating weeks and these men came from just down the road. One older barefoot gentleman dressed entirely in white sat at the door of the Balam Na, the Jaguar House, the place where the holy cross was now kept. Kneeling down on the ground next to him, I slowly and quietly spoke the short introductory words in Yukatek Maya that I had rehearsed in preparation for our visit. The shrine guard's reply was immediate and short: *"Ma'"* ("No"). Experience in the Mayan world had made me accustomed to the Mayan habit of feeling comfortable during silences in a conversation. I simply sat there quietly, completely willing to accept the elder's decision, while he closely observed my reaction. For a brief moment, our eyes met. *"Ma'alob"* ("OK"), said the guard without further explanation, motioning for us to leave our shoes outside the sacred space. *"Oken'ex"* ("Come in"), he urged.

The spacious room with a woven thatch roof was mostly empty apart from a few benches and an altar area set opposite the main entryway. The temple's altar was unlike any I had ever seen before. A large table stood in the front of the room with two bent wooden poles connecting the diagonal corners. The intersecting poles created crossed arches over the center of the table and were decorated with fresh flowers and hanging gourds. Standing on the table under the arches was some sort of object, perhaps two feet in height, covered with a cloth. Several men introduced themselves to us and inquired about our presence among them. One man in particular seemed intent on making sure we understood the significance of what we were seeing. I recall his saying that there was a cross underneath the cloth and that it remained covered for our own protection, to shield us from its potentially overwhelming power. Only during the ceremony about to take place would they unveil it.

We sat for perhaps an hour watching the preparations. One by one, barefoot men came in the temple door carrying offerings of food and slowly walked toward the holy altar at the front of the temple. In one hand, each held a small pot of beans still warm from their wives' cooking fires at home. In the other, they carried a beautifully wrapped stack of handmade tortillas fresh off the griddle, secured with a colorful bow. The genuine devotion on the faces of these followers of the Mayan cross revealed a profound respect. One man took all the offerings and placed them on a table set aside for that purpose near the altar. Before long, the entire table was filling up with food and it appeared that most of the men in this small community were inside the temple structure. I could not help but feel moved by the reverence of the assembled group and asked one of the men in charge if it would be acceptable for us to make an offering as well. He seemed amused by the idea. I then asked him, given that we had nothing besides our personal belongings, what would be an appropriate gesture to acknowledge our respect for their traditions. He suggested a case of Coke. I had avoided soft drinks for more than twenty-five years, so I could not help but feel amused by the personal irony of contributing Coca-Cola for a sacred ritual. Once the case of Coke had been added to the table of ritual offerings, one of the temple attendants removed the shroud from atop the cross, revealing a green effigy adorned with a miniature version of the white muslin dresses worn by local women. Simultaneously, the assembly dropped to its knees in prayer. Listening to the kneeling, barefoot men recite their prayers struck a chord deep within me. In the final analysis, this is what the Macewal Maya had fought and died for, to be able to make their humble offerings of sacred corn to the divine world that sustained them. Thousands had shed their blood in sacrifice so that these few could continue to practice their particularly Mayan way of experiencing their connection to the cosmos.

Alcohol as a Holy Substance

For outsiders, perhaps one of the least comprehensible aspects of Mayan spirituality is the ritual usage of alcohol. We often view the ingestion of liquor as antithetical to our spiritual lives and some go so far as to connect it with demonic influences. Whereas many of us are accustomed to the ritual use of wine in remembrance of the Last Supper, some Maya use alcohol as a spiritual tool to open themselves to a more full-hearted experience of the divine or as a means of healing.

My own first experience of ritual alcohol consumption came in a Tzotzil Mayan community in Chiapas, Mexico. In many Mayan languages, *tzotzil* is a reference to the "bat," an animal closely associated with the exploits of the Hero Twins in the *Popol Vuh* story. My young family and I had arrived in this highland town on the first bus, long before the groups of mostly European tourists would arrive from nearby San Cristóbal de las Casas. The town center seemed virtually empty at that early hour. The municipal offices were closed so we were unable to sign the mandatory form promising not to take any photos. Apparently, occasional rude tourists had made such stringent restrictions necessary. The small white church that sits at the heart of the town had just opened. As we passed the large wooden cross in front of the church, I noticed that it was painted in what the Tzotzil call *yox*, their language's variant of the "green" color of the cosmic tree, the Yax Te'. Just to make certain that the identification was clear, local officials had lashed freshly cut pine branches to the cross, emphasizing its symbolic value as a tree and not just an emblem of Christianity.

As we approached the church doorway, I steered our two children clear of an intoxicated man lying face down on the pavement who was oblivious to our passage. Unfortunately, I had seen many such scenes in the Mayan world, where distilled alcohol has sometimes had devastating effects on communities that, before the invasion of Europeans, consumed alcohol only in the form of mildly fermented corn beer or honey water, and even then usually in a ritualistic context. Having participated in hundreds of Roman Catholic Masses in dozens of churches, I was surprised to see that in this church, dedicated to St. John, there were no pews, nor did there appear to be any priests. Instead, the entirety of the floor space was several inches deep in freshly cut pine needles that exuded a delightful aroma usually experienced only in the deep forest. Individuals and groups of two or three people sat randomly in the church interior upon the pine needles praying and healing one another. My wife, two children, and I found our own space on the floor and sat quietly observing the activities around us. To one side, a man passed an egg over the body of a woman kneeling in front of a row of burning candles in a process that I later learned was for diagnostic purposes. Immediately to the other side of us, a middle-aged couple also had their own row of candles burning in a space they had cleared in the pine needles. The man was on his feet, his arms outstretched, reciting prayers between sips of what the Tzotzil call *pox*, a word for cane sugar liquor that means "remedy" or "medicine." He seemed to be in another world, one he had accessed through the *pox*. Tears streamed down his face as he called out to the divine, unburdening his heart while at the same time opening himself to the divine. Sitting slightly closer to us on the floor, the man's wife also sipped the holy liquor as she unraveled fresh candles from their newspaper wrappings. I could not help but notice her pause to examine one of the newspaper comics as she carefully peeled the paper from one of the candles before lighting it on the floor in front of her husband. As we looked around the room, most all of the participants seemed genuinely immersed in their spiritual pursuits, and all were deeply inebriated.

I approached a man at the door who seemed to be a church official and asked if it would be permissible for my family to participate as well. With my wife and kids waiting on the pine needles, he took me to a nearby storefront, where he helped me purchase enough candles and a small flask of "medicine." Back with my family, we passed the bottle between us, with our ten-year-old son and thirteen-year-old daughter barely touching the bottle and its stinging contents to their lips. After some time sipping the *pox,* I found myself getting more comfortable, leaning my head to the carpet of pine needles from our kneeling position. The uplifting scent was inspiring in itself, but the deeply reverent atmosphere and the blending of prayerful Tzotzil voices led me to an inner experience of profound devotion. A deep love for humanity arose within, facilitated by the Tzotzil "medicine." As we glided out through the church door toward the cobblestone plaza outside, we walked past the same resting man we had seen on the way in. I saw that his head was lying only a foot or two away from a tiny stream of sparkling clear water gurgling past from the surrounding mountains. In contrast to my earlier pity for the heavily inebriated man, I felt a twinge of envy for his ideal resting spot next to the soothing sounds of Mother Nature.

I encountered another example of ritualized alcohol consumption in the presence of a Mayan deity named Mam, a word that literally means both grandfather and father, but that figuratively refers to the ancestral spirit in general. Mam, more popularly known as Maximón, is a mannequin-like entity held to be sacred by some among the Tz'utuhil Maya who live on the shores of a massive crater lake in Guatemala known locally as Nim Ya, "Big Water." I had the good fortune to meet Mam in the company of a devotee from the United States who spoke Tz'utuhil and was very much a part of the local culture. We carried bales of pine needle flooring from my companion's forest home as a practical contribution to our collective comfort and as an offering to the "Ancient Ancestor," Rilaj Mam. Mam is a wooden embodiment of the divine, capable of continually shifting form as needed for his transformative work enriching human life. He can become an eye-catching beauty or an inquisitive skunk, a needy child or an abusive town official—whichever form functions best for teaching the necessary lessons in living. Those who follow Mam's ways maintain a focus for worshipping him in the form of a nearly human-size mannequin, ritually adorned and cared for by a small retinue of attendants. As we entered the ritual space with our bags of pine needles, friendly smiles greeted my eyes on all sides. Our hosts guided us to spots on the floor at the feet of Mam, whose figure sat roughly in the center of the small room, while several men spread the aromatic evergreen needles on the floor. The wooden face of Mam had a burning cigar in its mouth and numerous brightly colored handkerchiefs were tied around his neck. As a teacher at Stetson University, a school named for the famous hatmaker, I could not help but admire the handsome Stetson hat perched atop Mam's head. As we settled in, a man who appeared to be the main attendant raised a small bowl under the smoking sacred tobacco in Mam's mouth and gently tapped the cigar until the ash fell in. He then carefully removed the cigar, opened a bottle of the local liquor, and poured a bit into the hole in Mam's wooden face. After the Holy Boy, as he is also known, had had his fill, the bottle was passed around to the rest of us, each taking a healthy swig of the throat-burning liquid. After several rounds of alcohol with Mam, those in the room had become an even more gregarious bunch, further elevated in spirit by the ubiquitous pine fragrance. As if on cue, one man picked up a guitar and began to strum a devotional song in Tz'utuhil. I relaxed easily into an inner state of revelry, in awe of an ancient means of remembering the divine. The dire consequences of alcohol consumption, all too common in so many Mayan communities, seemed utterly irrelevant in the context of this sacred usage.

Cholq'ih: The 260-Day Ritual Calendar

Every dimension of Mayan life is held to be sacred. Even time has holy dimensions. According to one senior member of the Mayan cultural revitalization movement, his people's most significant contribution to spirituality and world civilization is their 260-day ritual calendar, most commonly known as the *tzolkin*. This fascinating method for interpreting time arises from a combination of the two numbers most significant to Mayan culture, thirteen and twenty. The number twenty formed the basis of their ancient numerical system. It also represents a complete human being, one with a full complement of ten digits on the hands and ten on the feet. In fact, the words for "twenty" and "human" are similar or identical in many Mayan languages. Likewise, several Mayan calendar priests have told me that the number thirteen refers to the human form with its thirteen principal articulations: ankles, knees, hips, wrists, elbows, shoulders, and neck. Multiplying the two "human" numbers of thirteen and twenty produces the number 260, the approximate number of days for human gestation. Although the practice is rare now, Maya used to name their children based on the day they were born in the *cholq'ih*. Maya reinforce the symbolic identification of human beings with corn by recalling that 260 days is also the approximate length of the Mayan agrarian year that begins in early February and ends in late October. According to the renowned anthropologist Barbara Tedlock, there is a variety of corn in the highlands that is harvested 260 days after planting.[6] Among the Tzeltal Maya, there are even thirteen named stages of corn production—not surprisingly, each twenty days in length.[7] Both maize and the human beings fashioned from corn dough by the ancient creator deities are born after passage through an identical period of 260 days.

Prudence Rice's brilliant analysis of the origins of the 260-day calendar goes even further by clarifying the numerous ties that the numbers thirteen, twenty, and 260 have in astronomy.[8] First, it must be recalled that near latitude 15 degrees north, precisely the area where Mayan calendars are thought to have originated, there are about 260 days between the summer solar zenith passage in August and the spring zenith passage at the beginning of May. Not coincidentally, the ancient Long Count calendar "zero" date occurred on the August 11 zenith passage, providing powerful reinforcement for the importance of the subsequent period of 260 days. Furthermore, according to Rice, the planet Venus is visible, either as the morning star or the evening star, for an average of 260 days. Yet another important astronomical link to Mayan sacred numbers can be found in relationship to the moon, known by the Mam Maya as *xhaw*, probably an abbreviated form of "female lord." This female lord of the night has a cycle of approximately twenty-nine days from full moon to full moon, a time period very close to the average human female's menstrual cycle. Significantly, the cycle of lunar phases includes a thirteen-day period of waxing (crescent to full moon) and a total of twenty days of lunar visibility. The remarkable 260-day *cholq'ih* calendar is a core feature of Mayan spirituality since it recalls many of the key natural components in the Mayan universe: the human body of twenty digits on its extremities and thirteen basic articulations, the period of human gestation, the agricultural cycle of maize, the sun's cycle between zenith passages, the two periods of Venus visibility, and even the phases of the moon.

The ritual calendar itself consists of twenty day-names. Each is an archetype with a well-developed set of meaning, symbolism, and connotations, all derived from the natural world. These names rotate sequentially in conjunction with the numerals 1–13, which also change daily. Thus, what practicing K'iche' daykeepers consider to be the first day, 8 Batz', is followed by 9 E', then 10 Ah, 11 I'x, and so on. Accordingly, the last day of this 260-day cycle for contemporary K'iche' is 7 Tz'i. Apart from the significance of 8 Batz' as a sort of Mayan new year, 13 Ahaw is perhaps the most revered of all Mayan dates since it combines the maximum numerical strength of thirteen with the auspicious qualities of Ahaw. Those Maya who still use this calendar in the highlands of Guatemala and Mexico believe that each day, with its corresponding number, has specific qualities and that a person born on that date will have tendencies based on those characteristics.

Below is a list of the Mayan ritual calendar day-names with those associations most often used by contemporary calendar priests. They are a compilation derived from numerous Mayan sources, including directly from active Mayan daykeepers. The day-names are in the K'iche' language with the oft-used Yukatek equivalent in parentheses. Those interested can calculate their own birth date on the 260-day calendar at www.michielb.nl/maya/calendar.html.

Imox (Imix) suggests watery beginnings, the primordial creation out of Mother Earth that, according to the *Popol Vuh,* arose from the all-encompassing seas. In fact, the sign itself resembles a seashell, perhaps the spiny *Spondylus* held sacred by the ancient Maya, with its sharp ridges and the red color associated with sacrificial blood and the east of the rising sun. It also suggests the spiny ridge on the back of a caiman, a creature from primal waters. Nature's creation pours forth with this day in the form of clouds, rains, natural springs, and rivers that find their way to estuaries and the sea herself, thus it is an auspicious day on which to pray for rain. According to daykeepers, those born on this day tend to be creative, energetic, receptive, protective, secretive, introspective, and even highly intuitive. They, like moving waters, can also be indecisive, dominating, unstable, deceptive, and turbulent. The day even can suggest mental illness and idiocy. The day is commonly associated with fish as well as with spiny-backed crocodilians and the thorny ceiba tree, symbol of cosmic creation. Those born on this day are said to have been conceived on the day Ah.

Iq' (Ik') is the day of wind. The moving air is the cosmic equivalent of human breath and voice. It also suggests the processes of initial movement and change. It can sweep life's road free of obstacles as well as bring both unforeseen calamity and new opportunities. Those born on the day Iq' are often idealistic, communicative, imaginative, and creative but can also experience an aversion to commitment, faithfulness, and responsibility and can be overly impulsive. Daykeepers link the day to the north with its cold winds and to the color white. It also relates to airborne materials such as dust, pollen, and spores, and suggests dryness as opposed to the moisture of the previous day. The "T" shape of the glyph for this day recalls the windows of the ancient Mayan temples that let in the outside air. The day is linked to the beautiful quetzal bird that rides the wind as it leaps from one tree to the next. Those born on this day are thought to have been conceived on I'x.

The day **Aq'abal** (Akabal) relates to darkness and the night but also strongly implies the impending dawn. Thus, the day suggests both nighttime introspection and anticipation of the morning light. It is both an end and a beginning. Daykeepers link the day to the underworld, where the absent sun dwells at night. The sign itself may represent a cave, the Earth's open mouth for the acceptance of offerings. In Mayan imagery, the sunlike, illuminated eyes of the jaguar at night, the lit cigar tips of the Hero Twins in the Dark House episode in the *Popol Vuh*, and the light of the morning star capture both the concepts of darkness and pending illumination conflated into this day. The day can be a good one for insights and divination, for seeking an appropriate mate, and for the mental clarity born from the hidden recesses of the soul. Those born on this day are powerful, sexually active, deep, conservative, and resistant, although they can also be mentally rigid and self-absorbed. True to its nighttime associations, black is the day's color and its direction is the west, where the sun goes down. Those born on this day are said to have been conceived on the day Tz'ikin.

K'at (Kan) has strong associations with netlike bindings and also with fire. The net symbolizes connections, the bonds that tie life together, and those that keep us captive. Most importantly, a net full of corn represents the gathering of human sustenance from the earth, an abundance of goods or goodwill. Conversely, the bindings of the net can also suggest entrapment. In human terms, the full net of corn takes symbolic form in the womb, and the day thus has strong associations with midwifery. The corn cycle ties the day to fire since Mayan farmers typically burn their fields prior to planting as a part of regenerating the sacred plant. The day also recalls the earth as a regenerative matrix for corn. These fiery and regenerative dimensions of this day give rise to individuals who are dynamic, sexual, and influential but who can also be unbalanced or sexually immature. The day's associations are with the south and with the golden yellow of ripe corn. The day is often associated with the lizard, and those born on this day are thought to have been conceived in Ahmaq.

Kan (Chikchan) is the day of the snake. As such, daykeepers associate it with the wise and just leadership of the mythical Plumed Serpent, K'uk'ulkan, the one who keeps balance between earth and sky. Not surprisingly, those born on this day often take leadership roles.

Ancient Mayan lords were often depicted with a serpent scepter in their hand, a powerful symbol of their political and spiritual power. They can be strong-willed, wise, and charismatic, but also they may be authoritarian, cruel, and extremist. They are prone to powerful emotions, such as anger, that can affect others as well as provoke intense internal transformations. The snake's coiled shape symbolically links the day to the spiraling cycles of Mayan time. The day's red color ties it to the rising sun in the east. The day is, of course, linked to the snake. Those born on this day were conceived in No'h.

A human skull represents **Kame** (Kimi), the day most associated with death. Often, when non-Maya learn that they were born on this day, they are horrified, not realizing that the Mayan understanding of death is far broader than our own. Rather than simply focusing on suffering and the end of our earthly existence, Maya link the day to the coming of a ripe old age and recollection of the beloved ancestors. More broadly, the day's meanings parallel the death process with suggestions of transformation, completion, serenity, and rest. On a social level, the day recalls the resolution of community conflict through the asking of pardon and the granting of forgiveness. Like the presence of death, this day can evoke humility and a deeper appreciation for life. In the interpersonal realm, it suggests attentiveness to the well-being of the community and a willingness to sacrifice on its behalf. The day corresponds to the north and the color white. Those born on this day were conceived in Tihax.

The day **Keh** (Manik) is the deer. Just as a deer's four hooves allow it to stand strong, this day is stable and powerful. The four supporting legs link the day to the four directions and, as such, it is a day for travel and walking. Those born on this day exhibit the qualities of generosity, happiness, peacefulness, and individualism. Like a deer, they can easily avoid problems and obstacles with their agility. While they can be nomadic and independent, they also have a cooperative spirit and a strong desire for close relations with others. The day has ties to sacrifice and ritual since the deer is a prey animal for the mighty jaguar, and the deer's hide often serves as a cover for the shaman's bundle of sacred objects. The deer has some negative connotations since one of its favorite foods is the Mayan farmers' corn, while it simultaneously serves as the guardian of the natural world untrammeled by agriculture. The day corresponds to the west and the darkness of black, when the deer generally feeds. The day's animal associations are with the deer. Those born on this day were conceived in Kawoq.

The day **Q'anil** (Lamat) relates to yellow corn and suggests its planting, the opening of the seeds, care for the cornfield, and the resulting abundance of this sacred crop. These positive associations make those born on this day energetic and playful, like well-fed human beings. Alternately, the day's active and exuberant qualities can lead to excess and a loss of self-control, producing troublesome individuals. The day's name is a derivative of the word for "yellow" and its orientation is toward the south. In Mayan culture, yellow suggests ripeness, thus the day implies maturity. The four-part sign itself recalls the four directions and, in particular, the four colors of corn. Those born on this day were conceived in Ahpub.

Toh (Muluk) is the day of payment and atonement. It recalls the sacrifice in which suffering takes place in the service of the community, thus reestablishing a natural balance. The sacrificial dimensions of the day and its red color link it to blood. Those born on this day are particularly imaginative and exhibit strong emotions, and thus are often romantic, psychic, or prone to fantasy. Their strong feelings can easily affect those around them. The day suggests pain, sickness, punishment, and debt. The day's direction is the east. Those born on this day were conceived in Imox.

Tz'i (Ok) is the day of the dog, and a stylized version of the animal's head sometimes functions as its sign. As such, the day relates to companionship, loyalty, protection, and collaboration. Those born on this day tend to have obstinate characters and often assume authority roles. With its keen senses, the dog gives this day associations with extraordinary intuition and perceptual capacities. Alternately, the day suggests animal passions, especially in terms of excessive sexuality. The dog's cousins, the coyote and fox, are alternate versions of this day. As such, they can be sly tricksters. The day points to the white of the north. Those born on this day were conceived in Iq'.

The day **Batz'** (Chuen) is the day of the howler monkey. In the *Popol Vuh*, the older brothers of the Hero Twins are monkeys and are artists, scribes, and musicians. As expressive and demonstrative personalities, they also relate to communication and writing. Like monkeys, those born on this day are curious, humorous, and attention-grabbing. Maya also see them as licentious and potentially self-indulgent. The day has an alternate meaning of "thread" and often represents a metaphorical filament of time that reaches back to the realm of the ancestors. The thread image also suggests the tying and untying of situations. The day is connected to the color black and to the west, where the sun enters darkness. Those born on this day were conceived in Aq'abal.

E' (Eb) traditionally relates to a tooth and has ties to sharpness and the figurative "bites" that life sometimes takes from us. The day has associations with sensitivity and carefulness as well as with practicality and usefulness. Those born on this day are easily hurt and are courteous about the feelings of others. More recently the day has also taken on the symbolism of the word *be,* which refers to the "road." The image of the road is an important one for the Maya and recalls both the real roads used for travel and the metaphorical road of life, one's destiny. The day refers to yellow and to the south. Those born on this day were conceived in K'at.

The day **Ah** (Ben) refers to a reed and is a powerfully positive day. Often associated with the rapidly growing cornstalk arising from a seed, the day symbolizes new growth and resurrection. The day implies knowledge of the body and its healing through intuition. Those born on this day are competent, talented, and fighters for principles. The day also relates to children, perhaps due to the image of a stalk arising from a kernel, just as a body emerges from tiny beginnings. The relationship the day has with children in turn links it with the home. Like a cornstalk, those born on this day can be rigid and they can sometimes grow too quickly, making them susceptible to harmful influences. The day points to the red of the east. Those born on this day were conceived in Kan.

I'x (I'x) is the day of the jaguar. As the region's top predator, the animal embodies the primal energy of the Earth and its sacred places. The day also represents magical powers arising from a highly developed and refined consciousness. The jaguar is the lord of the night and symbolizes the shaman's spiritual journey into the darkness of the underworld. Those born on this day have characteristics of the jaguar: they are silent, sensitive, intelligent, highly intuitive, and aggressive. They tend to avoid direct confrontation. The day suggests both internal and situational complexity and has connections with fear and warfare. It refers to the white north. The day is naturally associated with the jaguar. Those born on this day were conceived in Kame.

The day **Tz'ikin** (Men) refers to the bird. Recalling the priceless feathers of a quetzal bird, the day connotes wealth and good fortune. As a creature of the sky, it symbolizes freedom. In personality, this day can be escapist and ambitious. The day symbolizes both the bird's beauty and its augury value as a messenger. Those born on this day have a spiritual inclination but can also be demanding and critical. They can also rob us at night, stealing seeds from the cornfields. The day relates to the color black and the west. It is associated with the quetzal. Those born on this day were conceived in Keh.

Ahmaq (Kib) is a day for depression, remorse, confession, and forgiveness. It also has strong associations with the souls of the ancestors, especially those recently deceased who seek to rest in peace. Given the suffering linked with this day, those born on it are generally serious and profound. They are realistic and practical due to their hardening life experience but can also develop real wisdom and high values as a result. The day recognizes humanity's sinful nature, especially its pride, lust, and anger. At the same time, it implies that life's suffering will cleanse the soul. Yellow is its color and the south is its direction. Those born on this day were conceived in Q'anil.

No'h (K'aban) is the day of thought and experiential knowledge. Those born on this day are rational and intelligent. They know what one should do since they are particularly insightful due to their connection to the heart. These ties also allow for inspiration and artistic expression. They are prudent and wise, understanding and loving. No'h is closely linked to the Earth and the knowledge derived from living in harmony with nature's ways. The day has the color red and the east is its direction. Those born on this day were conceived in Toh.

The day **Tihax** (Etznab) recalls the obsidian blade of sacrifice. As such, it suggests danger, pain, and killing. It can be a day of conflict and harsh words. At the same time, this symbolic blade can cut limiting knots and quickly end bad situations. It can even refer to cutting out malignant aspects of our beings. Those born on this day tend to be analytical and rational, with strong mechanical inclinations. For those reasons, the day often has associations with work and building. The day refers to the white north. Those born on this day were conceived in Tz'i.

Kawoq (Kawaq) is a day of rain and is the most decidedly feminine day on the calendar. It is a powerful day linked with storms, lightning, and rainbows. The rains of Kawoq nourish the holy corn. Those born on this day are cooperative, friendly, and gossipy. They tend to be deeply spiritual. Since they readily get involved in the lives of others, they also have a great capacity as healers. Their facility with words gives them a special aptitude as both students and teachers. The day refers to the blackness of storm clouds and the approaching nighttime of the west. Those born on this day were conceived in *Batz'*.

Ahpub (Ahaw) is the culminating day of the ritual calendar and refers to the Lord and the sun. The day has ties to the hunting blowgunner, the guardian of corn. Those born on this day generally are loving, dedicated, and artistic, but they also can be dreamers who are inflexible and socially awkward. The day has ties to decapitation due to its association with both the father and son known as Ahpub in the *Popol Vuh* who lost their heads in their conflicts with the Lords of Death. The day has the color of yellow corn and south is its direction. Those born on this day were conceived in E'.

Respect

The intricacies of meaning and complex calculations of Mayan calendrics can seem daunting but Mayan spirituality is readily accessible since it is remarkably simple at its core. Several years ago I had the opportunity to visit among people from the three different Mayan language groups that live in Belize. I traveled with June and four of our best university students. Our Yukatek-speaking friend Patricio went with us and arranged a visit to his hometown in the Cayo District. One of the highlights of our time in this quaint Mayan community was a brief chat with one of his uncles, an octogenarian with a sharp sense of humor who seemed to take delight in our presence. As he relaxed in his hammock, he patiently responded to my students' questions and then, as the conversation quieted down, I saw an opportunity to probe beyond my students' inquiries into the practicalities of daily survival. I described what exceptional young people I had with me, their genuine commitment to bettering the world, their intelligence, and their boundless curiosity. Then I asked him, as an experienced human being, what advice he might have to offer these enthusiastic souls in terms of how to lead a satisfying life. After Patricio translated my words into Yukatek, his uncle responded almost reflexively and succinctly, "Respect." He said that was all that was needed: respect for nature, respect for other people, respect for God. Whereas New Agers like me tend to get caught up in the study of esoteric traditions, complex analyses of sacred scripture, and even probing cosmic symbolism related to 2012, Maya themselves have little time or interest in such pursuits and tend to orient their spirituality around simply honoring life itself.

Not long ago, an especially dear Mayan friend of ours sat outside under a tree on the Stetson University campus where I teach, giving students in my Mayan Culture class an introductory lesson in weaving. It was a glorious Florida spring day and while she focused on her intricate brocade work, she began interjecting expressions of gratitude for the day into her weaving descriptions. She expressed her appreciation for the warmth of the sun, for her grandmother who had taught her to weave, and for her children. As she continued, tears welled up in her dark eyes and she quietly murmured, *"Gracias, Diosito lindo"* ("Thanks, dear beautiful God"). When she spoke these words, in a gesture that may have gone unnoticed by my students, her hand went from the batten on her loom to touch the earth in front of her, scoop up a tiny amount of the sandy soil with her fingers, and then quickly release it. This spontaneous, nonideological, experientially derived and highly physical sense of humble appreciation forms the very heart of Mayan spirituality. This genuine respect for nature, for our human brothers and sisters, and for the living cosmos itself is the fundamental lesson from Maya to the outside world and a gift from their culture that we can cherish in this era of 2012.

CHAPTER 8

The Mayan World and the Eco-apocalypse: Time for Reflection

Mayan author and cultural activist Gaspar González with Q'anjobal Mayan priest.

Who Are the Maya?

Many involved in the 2012 phenomenon depict the Maya as being remote in both time and space, an ancient and exotic civilization that apparently collapsed and disappeared in the tropical forests of Middle America more than a thousand years ago. Some say the Maya came in ancient times from stars light-years away and returned to their celestial abode long ago. However, in truth, the ancient Maya never left the planet or died out. When Mayan city-states failed in the ninth century, the survivors ventured farther north into the Yucatán

Peninsula or journeyed south, ascending into the highlands of modern-day Guatemala and Chiapas. Others believe the Mayan people died out from disease and violence after the invasion of the Spanish conquistadors in the early 1500s. Although it may be true that the Mayan population was reduced by as much as 90 percent in the period following the conquest, Maya still persisted in large numbers and then their population rebounded significantly, recovering to its preconquest levels by the mid-twentieth century. In fact, the some eight million Maya alive today make up a total indigenous population not seen in this region for more than a millennium. Tens of thousands of Maya even live among us, outside of their ancestral homelands, hidden among Latino immigrants from south of the U.S.-Mexican border, most seeking a better life for their beloved families back home. Not only did the Maya not disappear in ancient times, they are not a physically distant society. Most people in the eastern United States actually live closer to the Mayan world than they do to the entire western part of our own country. Rather than being distant and vanquished, the Maya are a thriving group of people with an intensely vital culture who are extremely diverse in language and beliefs. They are our hardworking neighbors who are currently attempting to reassert and re-create their own traditions in the context of exceedingly rapid social and environmental changes that are transforming the Mayan region.

Maya are probably most familiar to the outside world as the creators of the ancient civilization that flourished for hundreds of years in the Mesoamerican lowlands of modern-day Guatemala, southeast Mexico, Belize, Honduras, and El Salvador, and then fell victim to a generalized societal collapse produced by environmental degradation in the ninth and tenth centuries. In recent decades, thanks to the work of dedicated scholars in the field of Mayan Studies working with contemporary Maya and studying their languages, the ancient hieroglyphic writing system has been largely deciphered. As a result, understanding of ancient Mayan society has expanded exponentially. During what archaeologists call the Classic Period of Mayan culture, roughly from 250 to 900 CE, elaborately attired shaman-kings ruled over dozens of powerful city-states, forging alliances and waging battle with lesser lords in relatively independent Mayan centers spread across the political landscape of the region. Two kingdoms in particular were dominant and struggled against one another over the course of the centuries. Calakmul, which was likely known originally as Uxte'tun, may have been the largest of all Mayan cities, covering more than eleven square miles in what is now the Mexican state of Campeche. Its main competitor, only three days' walk to the south in modern Guatemala, was the spectacular city of Yax Mutal, known to modern tourists as Tikal.

Each kingdom had a ruler, most frequently known as an *ahaw*, or "lord," who on special occasions ceremonially performed self-sacrifice, drawing precious blood from his or her own body using sharp instruments such as stingray spines and obsidian blades in rites meant to provide visionary encounters with their ancestral spirit guides. As it is today, direct and personal experience of the divine was at the heart of ancient Mayan life. Depictions of the sacrificial offering of the *ahaw's* blood for accessing visions are found throughout the region's ancient ruins, carved into the soft limestone slabs or painted on elaborate stucco murals that decorate especially important Mayan temples. Ancient Maya considered this vital fluid to be so sacred that its sacrifice might be a sufficiently dear payment to bring about a divine response. The Classic Mayan word *k'uhul* is a reference to the divine and appears prefixed to the hieroglyphic name of many Classic Period rulers in the logographic form of cascading droplets of blood. Just as contemporary traditional Mayan priests currently prepare for *costumbre*, the Spanish name for their sacred ceremonies, an ancient *ahaw* probably fasted for several days, sweated intensely in the moist heat of a purifying sauna, abstained from sex for an extended period, and became immersed in inner concentration in anticipation of the bloodletting. Through these rigorous measures, the *ahaw* could attain an exceptionally sensitive physical condition as well as a finely receptive psychological state. This ritual may have been profoundly enhanced by the ingestion of psychoactive substances such as "magic" mushrooms or the DMT mentioned in Chapter Two that is derived from the glands of the large *Bufo marinus* toads that still can be seen lumbering lazily across the rainforest floor near Mayan ruins sites. The culminating act of penetrating a tender part of the body with a sharp instrument may have served as a final catalyst, pushing the *ahaw* beyond the patterns of the normal waking state into a profoundly altered state of consciousness and, perhaps, a visionary trance. Mayan illustrations from this period show ancestral spirits emerging from the smoke of the burned, blood-stained paper lying on the floor in front of the *ahaw*. The remarkably serene faces of these sacrificing Mayan leaders seen on the Classic Period temple walls suggest that they cultivated states of consciousness that may have transcended pain, much as modern shamans do in the Philippines, India, and elsewhere who pierce their bodies with sharp objects while in ecstatic trance states without experiencing apparent physical or psychological trauma.

Classic Period iconography sometimes seems to make a parallel between the *ahaw*'s sprinkling of individual droplets of sacrificial blood from his male member and the casting out of sacred kernels of maize into Mother Earth. Both the ancient lords and Mayan farmers, past and present, are "planting" for the benefit of their people. Maya grew their highly prized corn in surprising abundance using ingenious agricultural practices capable of extracting impressively bountiful crops from the lowlands' notoriously poor soils. Their fine arts blossomed in the form of exquisite ceramics, sculpture, painting, architecture, and intricately shaped ceremonial blades flaked from volcanic glass. Using an elaborate hieroglyphic system that had hundreds of aesthetically pleasing and intricately stylized signs, Maya were one of the few people in the New World who employed writing much as we do, to record their own history and inscribe their understanding of the cosmos.[1] The ancient Mayan hieroglyphic texts and iconography reveal a worldview in which all aspects of the universe were understood as divine emanations. Growing corn was a holy endeavor as well as a physical necessity and was even practiced by the gods themselves in the *Popol Vuh*, the K'iche' Mayan sacred text. The elaborately carved doorways and lofty pyramid platforms of ancient Mayan architecture functioned as stone re-creations of the most revered spaces in nature, the portal openings of caves and towering summits of mountain peaks, places on the landscape held holy as special access points to the Heart of Earth and Heart of Sky, respectively. Even warfare and political strife, just as common among ancient Maya as in our modern world, frequently appear depicted as flowing from cosmic processes, with military assaults timed to coincide with specific planetary movements and victories celebrated with reverential ceremony. Unlike the deliberately barbaric and crude depiction of the Maya in Mel Gibson's film *Apocalypto*, warfare was a highly ritualized affair and focused on the capture of an enemy's leaders rather than merely inflicting casualties on civilians or capturing them for mass sacrifice.

Besides leaving a record of the military and spiritual exploits of their shamanic rulers, ancient Mayan scribes filled their almanacs with a remarkable record of astronomical movements in astonishing precision. In Mayan iconography, celestial bodies often took symbolic forms that acted out complex mythologies involving celestial animal deities and supernatural beings. A few investigators follow the late Mayanist Linda Schele in believing that Maya gave particular attention in their iconography to our home galaxy, the Milky Way, which, absent the visual "pollution" of our artificial lighting, appeared to them as a white band stretching across the pitch-black, star-adorned night sky. According to Schele, in their artwork, Mayan artists sometimes represented the Milky Way in the form of a magnificent tree referred to as the Yax Te', the "first/green tree." Across this galactic tree symbol lay a band with serpent heads at both ends that may have symbolized the ecliptic arc, the apparent pathway followed by the sun and planets across the heavens. Some researchers claim that Mayan astronomers at the Guatemalan site of Quiriguá even intuitively pinpointed what they saw as the creation site of the cosmos near Orion's Belt, a place where modern scientists tell us is, in fact, the brightest and nearest place of star creation in the northern sky, the Orion Nebula.

Ironically, and perhaps with acute relevance to humanity's current global environmental crisis, the amazing "success" of the Classic Period Maya provides a partial explanation for their society's collapse, a gradual process that took place primarily in the ninth century. Mayan agricultural genius produced enough food to allow for growing population levels that gradually depleted the topsoil and used up ever greater amounts of their most crucial resource, wood. Just as we moderns are vitally reliant on petroleum and its by-products, the world of the Classic Maya had a multifaceted dependence on trees. Maya used wood for heating the rocks in their saunas for bathing. They required it to prepare their sacred corn for daily meals and it was needed for building family dwellings and making tools. Significantly, "consumption" of the tropical forest was required for "cooking" limestone to produce lime, the key adhesive ingredient in the mortar and stucco used in the creation of all of their masonry structures, including the major Mayan architectural monuments. The increasingly widespread removal of the cloud-producing forest cover in the Mayan lowlands combined with long-term regional climatic cycles to produce a series of droughts, the most severe period of low rainfall in the area in some seven thousand years.[2] The success of the intensive and diversified Mayan agricultural system in the lowlands was critically dependent on a consistent water level since in these generally flat conditions, even a slight drop in water level can leave large artificially irrigated fields bone dry. With recurrent drought, a true ecological disaster gradually spread across the region over the course of many decades. The lack of rain, of course, implied a lack of food and other vital resources. This led to intensified and spreading warfare between the competing alliances of ancient Mayan cities. Maya gradually abandoned nearly all their principal centers, and the survivors of this environmental disaster sought refuge in redeveloping communities in the northern plains of the Yucatán Peninsula and in the mountainous highlands to the south.

Mayan civilization endured a second cataclysmic period in the sixteenth century with the arrival of Spanish invaders fresh from their defeat of the last Islamic kingdom in the Iberian Peninsula and the forced expulsion of their Jewish population in 1492. Spaniards disembarked in the Western Hemisphere with a fury at the height of the most xenophobic period in their history. During this ugliest chapter in Spanish history, so-called Christians had forced the Iberian Peninsula's Jews and Moslems into exile or involuntary conversion with widespread use of torture and public executions by fire. With the fanatical zeal of conquering crusaders, the Spaniards crushed Mayan resistance on the battlefield with vastly superior arms, sadistic cruelty, extreme treachery, and effective manipulation of inter-Mayan rivalries. Without resistance to many European diseases, and living under the deliberately severe oppression of their Spanish masters, Maya experienced extreme and unprecedented suffering that may have exceeded the horrors experienced during the collapse of their Classic Period civilization. Smallpox, typhus, measles, and influenza—diseases previously unknown in the New World—became pandemic. As nursing Mayan mothers died, so did their precious infants. As hardworking corn farmers perished, so did the families that depended on them. Due to their relative frailty, the deeply revered elders nearly all died, carrying with them elements of the experiential wisdom acquired over countless generations. During the first century and a half after the Spanish invasion, the Mayan population plummeted by more than 80 percent. This apocalyptic scenario repeated itself across the hemisphere during this period as millions of Native Americans perished in what may be humanity's most horrific episode of mass death.

The devastation brought about by the European arrival was so severe that the Mayan population returned to its preinvasion levels only some four centuries later. The scope of this second tragedy in Mayan culture is difficult to fathom but the impact of this period on the Mayan collective psyche is evident. While I believe that the almost reflexive respect for nature in the contemporary Mayan world arose from its tragic experience with environmental collapse at the end of the Classic Period, I think that their already passionate reverence for elders and ancestors also intensified and reaffirmed itself in response to this postconquest period of near annihilation. One can almost imagine the survivors' daily trips to the cemetery to bury their dead. The death of their beloved family—the ancient ones, the grandfathers and grandmothers, the *mam*—still seems always present in the minds of their modern descendants.

Besides their time-tested ability to survive, an advantage that Maya enjoyed relative to other native peoples during the colonial period was their relative lack of resources considered valuable by the voraciously greedy Spanish invaders. The metal-hungry Spaniards flocked to the silver- and gold-laden mountains of Mexico and the Andes to sack the riches of their new Aztec and Incan subjects, leaving areas like the Mayan homeland in relative isolation after the initial onslaught of conquest. Apart from Spanish administrative strongholds in Antigua Guatemala, Mérida, and Campeche, the Spanish presence in the Mayan area was numerically minimal and, at least in terms of daily life, Mayan ways gradually reasserted themselves.

In Guatemala, this relative calm for the Maya ended in the late nineteenth century when so-called Liberal reformers, determined to set the country on a capitalistic course, set up large plantations for the production of coffee and cotton. Agribusiness success required massive landholdings, cheap labor, and a transportation infrastructure. Through their control of the national government, emergent capitalist interests managed to obtain all three from the Maya. The Guatemalan government abolished much of communally held Mayan landownership, allowing the fertile lands of the coastal piedmont to pass into private, white, wealthy hands. It also forced many Maya into the labor force, some working for pathetic wages under contract on the plantations, others as indentured servants, and still others slaved in miserable conditions simply with the promise of future pay. Local governments managed requests for forced labor, in which the Maya worked from a week to a month each year, either on the plantations or on transportation infrastructure projects. The system got even worse in the 1930s when, in yet another effort to give business interests access to inexpensive labor, Guatemala imposed vagrancy laws that required those without jobs to work between 100 and 150 days each year on government and private projects. Since most Maya were subsistence farmers, working full-time to grow food for their own families, this meant that authorities could legally force thousands of Maya into virtual slavery. Anyone who has worked even for a day with a typical Mayan subsistence farmer can appreciate the extreme irony of forcing these people, probably some of the most industrious on our planet, to work because of being officially "vagrants."

As the population recovered in the twentieth century, it briefly looked as though the future of many Guatemalan Maya might actually improve when a university professor named José Arévalo came to power in 1944. A genuine reformer and civic servant, the new Guatemalan president promoted a progressive social agenda that, perhaps for the first time since the conquest, gave the well-being of the majority Mayan citizens at least some consideration. This short experiment in popular democracy came crashing down in 1954 when U.S. business and political interests, in the form of the United Fruit Company and the Central Intelligence Agency, came into conflict with the reformist Guatemalan government. The U.S. corporation had massive landholdings in Guatemala and close connections with leaders in the CIA and State Department. Much of the land was cultivated for banana production while additional properties remained in reserve for future use. When the elected government requested to purchase these lands for use by land-starved Mayan farmers, it offered an amount based on land values used by the banana company itself for tax purposes, a figure that, for obvious reasons, was set unrealistically low. In order to protect the business interests of this U.S. company, the United States charged that the Guatemalan civilian government was communist and sponsored a military coup that led to decades of brutal dictatorship and a third Mayan apocalypse. Highlighting our government's involvement in the military takeover, the first of many repressive dictators supported by the United States flew into Guatemala City inside the U.S. ambassador's private airplane.

Before long, nationalist disgust with the Guatemalan military dictatorship's servile attitude toward U.S. interests stirred internal dissension among young officers in the Guatemalan army and eventually led to the establishment of a splinter group that began a guerrilla campaign against the government in the 1960s. When the military brutally crushed this internal rebellion, the surviving guerrilla leaders shifted operations into the largely Mayan western highlands in hopes of gaining support from the indigenous population. In the 1970s, as some Maya began to join the ranks of the guerrillas, Guatemala's military and the economic elite began to feel threatened by the potential of a revolutionary uprising among the nation's Native American majority. No doubt, the greatest fear of the white minority ruling in the Mayan highlands was, and remains, that this majority population might rise up against its traditional oppressors. In a drastic and misdirected policy that began in the late '70s, the Guatemalan army launched a war deliberately targeting Mayan civilians, thus hoping to annihilate any chance of an indigenous rebellion by eliminating its potential base of support. Tens of thousands of Maya died in numerous massacres that included large numbers of women and children as victims. In 1982, a delusional evangelical general, strongly supported and admired by President Reagan, staged an internal coup and further escalated the military campaign with still greater numbers of civilian Mayan deaths.

Many have written about this attempted genocide but words are wholly inadequate to do justice to the depth of the horror. When we know of the relentless nurturing of Mayan mothers nursing their precious babies, the Mayan community's quiet respect for its wise elders, the Mayan love of nature, and their humble and spontaneous awe for the divine, the thought of these gentle souls dying at the hands of brutish generals leaves us at a loss for words. Although Maya do verbalize this unbearable sorrow, the more common expression is simply to weep. Tears well in the eyes of a village elder as he recalls his dear son, tortured and executed by the army after false accusations made by a jealous neighbor that he had aided the "communist" subversives. A middle-aged man's body quivers as he remembers the death of an infant son, unable to endure the hardships as he and his family fled for their lives, walking through the jungle into exile in Mexico. A drunken Mayan man staggers from one pew to the next during a rural church service, weeping profusely, leaning on the parishioners for support as they glance at him with understanding eyes. Never does anyone ask him to leave. An elder gentleman whispers gently in his ear, gently touching his hand, eliciting even more heart-wrenching sobs. When I inquire after the service about what I had seen, people tell me that the crying man had been forcibly conscripted by the army, trained to hate his own people, and murdered many innocents before returning to his mountain home in a desperate search for peace. Maya have shed millions of tears in recent decades, moistening the holy earth with their sorrow, watering the bones of their beloved already departed from the surface of the Earth

When the military's slaughter finally spent itself, nearly two hundred thousand civilian Maya were dead or missing, and hundreds of thousands more had fled on foot into exile to Mexico and beyond. Several hundred Mayan communities had vanished entirely, burned to the ground. To get a sense of the scale of this third Mayan apocalypse, a proportional number of deaths in the contemporary United States would leave some ten million Americans dead. Even though the Guatemalan government and the leftist guerrillas signed a peace accord in 1996 formally ending this Mayan nightmare, the wounds are still fresh for many Maya, and military oppression remains lurking in the shadows. Complicating matters further, many of the army conscripts who killed Mayan villagers, like the sobbing man in the church mentioned above, were Maya themselves. The army regularly rounded up native boys in highland villages at gunpoint, kidnapping them into anti-Mayan military indoctrination and combat against other Maya, leaving many as tortured souls struggling to reintegrate into community life.

In Mexico, Maya have faced challenges of violent racism and extreme oppression similar to those of their indigenous brothers and sisters in Guatemala. In the nineteenth century, the Mexican government brutally put down a mass uprising of Yukatek Mayan farmers known as the Caste War. As in twentieth-century Guatemala, Mexican Mayan villagers died by the tens of thousands and the total population of the Yucatán Peninsula dropped by 40 percent in just four years.[3] In the Mexican highlands in the state of Chiapas, Maya have for the most part avoided mass slaughter, in spite of several serious indigenous attempts at armed rebellion. Nevertheless, the Spanish-speaking minority has historically treated Maya as less than human. Only since 1994, with the quasi-military support of the grassroots Zapatista movement ostensibly led by Subcomandante Marcos, the Mayan communities in Chiapas have been able to force some openings in the extremely repressive social environment.

Maya as Our Neighbors

Maya form, by far, the largest Amerindian cultural nexus in North America. In spite of their massive numbers and the close proximity of the Mayan world to the United States, however, there was minimal interaction between these two cultural realms before John Lloyd Stephens' tales of spectacular and mysterious pyramids lost in the Mesoamerican jungles piqued the reading U.S. public's interest in 1843.[4] Apart from a bloody incursion to help massacre rebel Maya five years later by mercenaries from the United States during the Caste War,[5] contact between the two cultures in the following century was largely limited to brief visits in the region by U.S. businessmen, diplomats, and academic researchers. As Central America became even more crucial to U.S. economic and political interests over the following decades, the United States' involvement in Guatemala increased further, at least in terms of support for the ruling alliance between the tiny Central American nation's military and its European-oriented elite. The devastating 1976 earthquake and the Guatemalan civil war slaughter of Mayan civilians marked the start of greatly intensified intercultural exchange as hundreds of thousands of Maya sought refuge and better economic opportunities in the United States and, as the violence abated, travelers from the United States came to the Mayan area in unprecedented numbers as tourists, aid workers, missionaries, and researchers.

Now, as the Mayan population surpasses eight million, this intriguing culture shares a broad, deep, and multifaceted interface with that of the United States. Millions of U.S. citizens and hundreds of thousands of Maya have traveled back and forth between the Mayan homelands and the U.S. mainland. In fact, uncounted hundreds of thousands of Maya now actually live and work in the United States both as legal and illegal immigrants. At the developing intersection between U.S. and Mayan cultures, unique phenomena have arisen that reflect the diverse interests and circumstances of those in each population.

New Agers contemplate the implications of their Dreamspell calendar status as so-called "Blue Monkeys," assuming incorrectly that they are tapping into the ancient roots of Mayan culture. Meanwhile, Mayan linguists in Guatemala and Yucatán study to be scribes in their own ancient hieroglyphic system under the guidance of academic experts in Mayan epigraphy from around the planet. A Tzotzil Mayan family at their weekly trip to market in San Cristóbal de Las Casas in the Chiapas highlands enjoys late-'60s songs from Sly and the Family Stone on their giant boom box as they shop for pitch pine kindling to get their fires started more easily in the moist, cool weather of July. Just across the border in Guatemala, a U.S. expat wearing traditional Mayan clothing toils in his Cuchumatán mountain cornfield as he chats in fluent Mam with a passing community elder who has stopped by to say hello. Farther west, waiting for an old Blue Bird school bus, the standard form of public transportation in highland Guatemala, at the bustling crossroads called Tres Caminos, a K'iche' Mayan man proudly dons his new Cleveland Indians warm-up jacket bearing the cartoon caricatured Native American face of Chief Wahoo on the back, hoping to keep out the early morning cold and turning on its head a U.S. sports image that emerged from callous racism. Back in the States, a white family plays gleefully with its giggling, newly adopted Mayan baby, wondering about who the baby's mother is and what the culture their new child has left behind forever is like. A Yukatek friend of mine, his last name revealing his "regal" status as a member of the House of the Jaguar, writes newspaper articles about a brutal mass murder arising from a dispute in the Florida suburbs over video games. A Mam widow, admired at home for her masterful weaving artistry, struggles as a migrant worker in the United States to send money home to her children and endures the anti-Indian scorn of her Mexican coworkers while mainstream Americans dismiss her as part of the Latino underclass. Such seemingly incongruent scenes give only the slightest hint of the richness, irony, and complexity found in the rapidly developing set of interactions between wildly contrasting cultural paradigms.

Perhaps the most significant participants in the Maya-U.S. cultural interface are the Maya who have migrated to the United States to avoid political violence or, more frequently in recent years, to seek better economic opportunities. During the unspeakable horrors of the Guatemalan civil war, tens of thousands of Maya, principally from the far-northwestern highlands, escaped on foot into remote areas in the Mexican state of Chiapas. Some of these people eventually made their way to the United States, as depicted in the highly acclaimed film *El Norte*. These war refugees have had an especially strong impact in towns like Lake Worth and Indiantown in Florida, where the Q'anhobal Maya have become, by far, the state's largest Native American population, far outnumbering the better-known Seminoles, another band of refugees who escaped slaughter, in this case at the hands of the United States Army, in the 1800s. Currently, hundreds of thousands of Maya have wagered their future, "investing" in a Mexican coyote system that takes them on the grueling and dangerous journey north to dismal jobs in cities and towns all over the United States. Maya from the Guatemalan highlands and elsewhere slaughter chickens in North Carolina to supply our "Auschwitz for animals"–based fast-food industry, harvest tomatoes in the pesticide-laden fields of south Florida, mix mortar in San Francisco Bay Area construction sites, and butcher cows in horrifically depressing beef processing plants.

Maya have earned a well-deserved reputation in the United States for being outstanding workers, as a natural consequence of their physically arduous lifestyle in high-altitude cornfields, and as contract laborers on cotton and coffee plantations in their homeland. Typically, assuming they have fulfilled their financial obligations to their coyotes, Mayan workers send most of their hard-earned money home to their families through a variety of private remittance services. These remittances have increased so rapidly that they are now principal sources of national income in both Guatemala and Mexico. In general, language barriers and their precarious legal status have effectively kept Maya from integrating into the U.S. mainstream. The predominance of Hispanic culture in the migrant labor population in the United States further isolates Maya since Hispanics generally have minimal appreciation for or knowledge of indigenous cultures. They, like most in our society, rarely identify or recognize Mayan laborers as Native Americans and are generally unaware of the Mayan presence among us. Instead, our society usually groups foreign Native Americans along with the Spanish-speaking Latinos from Mexico and elsewhere, making the Maya largely invisible within the U.S. underclass. Latinos, known by Maya deprecatingly as Ladinos, are a group that Maya have historically experienced as aggressively hostile. Mayan laborers struggling for their families' survival back at home have little choice other than to set aside this bitter irony.

Many Maya have become gravely concerned about the plight of these workers who have abandoned their psychological and physical ties to their ancestral homeland and to the Earth itself. One Mayan elder voiced his apprehensions to me after spending the morning gazing into the faces of drug-addled Mayan adolescents on the streets of Lake Worth, Florida. Accustomed to the friendly yet respectful banter he enjoyed among young people in Mayan villages in Guatemala, he was stunned by the glassy-eyed stares and physical immobility of Mayan teenagers lying on the cracked pavement. His kind voice and gentle touching of their hands brought little response beyond occasional surprise that someone was attempting to communicate with them. He marveled with tears in his eyes that these young people's parents had gone to so much effort to escape death at the hands of the

Guatemalan army only to have their children, estranged from their ancestral mountain communities, suffer from the abuse of substances previously unknown in the Mayan world.

The Q'anhobal Mayan elder and novelist Gaspar González has expressed a similar preoccupation, using the metaphor of a severed umbilicus between such Mayan expatriates and their ancestral lands to describe the plight of many Maya living far from home. Activists within Mayan communities in the United States have formed organizations to promote indigenous cultural values and community health awareness in response to a widely perceived sense that their ancestral cultural paradigm is disintegrating within the soulless underbelly of U.S. consumer culture.

This concern for Mayan culture's survival in the United States mirrors intense apprehension in the Mayan rural communities of Guatemala and Mexico about the modern influences arriving with friends and relatives returning home from their sojourn to the north. Village elders regularly bemoan the "lack of respect" among those whom they see as having been corrupted by the ways of the United States. University-educated Mayan cultural revivalists express similar concerns regarding what they see as a matter of spiritual survival. In the words of one, "Each day we lose more of our profound respect toward Mother Nature, respect toward our elders, and reverence toward the dead."[6] Returning Mayan workers bring home radically different values, and these relatively wealthy returnees find that their foreign experience accords them some measure of respect among their peers as well as a personal sense of accomplishment. The presence of these "America savvy" Maya back home in their communities combines with the effects of corporate advertising that now reaches virtually every hamlet in the Mayan world, hawking everything from junk food to toxic pesticides. The results have been powerfully transformative. On the plus side, Mayan women use cell phones to stay in touch with their husbands in the United States, easing the pains of family separation, and Mayan children are learning to read and gaining far greater access to accurate information concerning the outside world. But simultaneously, Mayan kids are beginning to hang out after school in video arcades instead of mastering the intricate and challenging textile skills of their culture such as weaving and crochet. In their fields, Maya increasingly grow culturally incongruent cash crops such as broccoli and ferns for export to the United States, virtually bathing themselves in modern agricultural chemicals, largely unaware of the dangers posed to local ecosystems and their own families. A few hybrid strains of Midwestern U.S. corn increasingly displace what was once an astonishing genetic diversity that included hundreds of heirloom strains, developed patiently by traditional Mayan farmers over thousands of years. Throughout the Mayan world, plastic food wrappers have now replaced corn husks and plant leaves for packaging, and this nearly indestructible trash accumulates in the streams and ravines as farmers till it into cornfields once regarded as holy. After surviving a catastrophic environmental and societal collapse over a millennium ago, the ravages of epidemic and slaughter wrought by the Spanish conquistadors, and genocidal wars in both Yucatán and Guatemala, Mayan culture may now face its gravest threat in relatively "harmless" forms such as video games, industrial chemicals, junk food, and other "advances" of the modern global lifestyle.

In most contemporary Mayan communities, women far outnumber men since males make up the vast majority of those who journey north to the United States and elsewhere looking for work. Increasingly, Mayan women must assume both male and female roles in both family and societal settings, as they become, for most practical purposes, heads of single-parent households. The results of this significant shift in gender roles are difficult to predict, but it may prove to be even more significant to the Maya than the recent mass conversions to evangelical Christianity initiated by aggressive missionaries from the United States. Women's numerical superiority combines with their long-standing informal role as guardians of cultural tradition to provide a basis for a disproportionately strong female influence in shaping the future of the Mayan world.

In Guatemala, there now exists a Mayan cultural revitalization movement known as the Movimiento Maya. It has roots in the 1940s that eventually flowered in post–civil war Guatemala, serving as a counterbalance to the perceived weakening of Mayan cultural values. To a lesser extent, this rekindled appreciation of indigenous ways has spread to Mayan communities in Mexico and Belize as well as to expatriate Maya living in the United States. The movement has roots firmly established in Amerindian soil. However, diverse foreign influences have helped to nurture its growth. These outsiders include Western academics, socially committed tourists, missionaries, and even participants in New Age spirituality.

Many in the leadership of the Mayan Movement come from the academic realm, especially from the social sciences, and they are often far more urban-oriented than the general Mayan population. A large number are linguists and sociologists, since the repressive Guatemalan military did not consider these intellectual domains to represent a significant threat to their rule. Until recent years, few Maya had access to higher education, and these professionals possessed only a distant, and highly moderated, voice in academic portrayals of their world. Increased educational opportunities and the end of the Guatemalan civil war provided a space for active indigenous scholarly participation. These new Mayan voices quite naturally challenged the legitimacy of existing foreign scholarship on the Maya, offering what they felt to be a more authentic representation of their own worldview. Scholarship by the Maya themselves has consequently tended toward seeing their own cultural paradigm as the primary resource for addressing their social and political issues. Meanwhile, even though academics in the United States generally reject what they view as essentialism on the part of Mayan scholars, they nearly all have adopted a stance of strong advocacy in support of Mayan social causes and have tended to place a premium on the value of Mayan perspectives.

In particular, Western scholars in Mayan Studies such as the late epigrapher Linda Schele have made deliberate efforts to include and valorize the Maya and Mayan perspectives in their academic research.

In fact, breakthroughs during recent decades in the decipherment of the ancient Mayan hieroglyphic system were possible only through a deepened understanding of contemporary Mayan languages and more substantive appreciation of Mayan ways. Schele and several other prominent academics have also made a point of sharing the results of their work with groups of Mayan cultural activists. She and others have conducted workshops on the glyphs in both Guatemala and Mexico for Maya from a variety of ethnic groups. As a consequence, Mayan cultural revivalists increasingly use components of the hieroglyphic system in their logos and other key aspects of their publications. For the first time since xenophobic Christians systematically destroyed Mayan writing in the sixteenth century, Mayan scribes have figuratively taken up their brushes and inkpots, in the form of digitized glyphs on their computers, in support of their ancient culture's very survival.

This Mayan renaissance may now embrace the possibilities inherent in the "change of era" thinking tied to 2012 to advance a pronative shift in regional affairs. A Mayan president in Guatemala might become a real possibility if majority Mayan voters become convinced that a change foretold in some way by their revered ancestors is about to unfold. Maya have already experienced massive societal "apocalypses" on more than one occasion and still live with vivid memories of bloody massacres of Mayan civilians by military dictatorships. Their culture has been deeply shaped by this catastrophic history. Mayan respect for nature is just one consequence of this tragic history.

Eco-apocalypse

Even if we completely dismiss the significance of 2012, one must admit that it is a great "coincidence" that its timing does, in reality, coincide with degrees and types of environmental degradation never before experienced by humanity. In many real ways, the world as we humans have known it since the beginning of our species really *is* ending. Our planet is now home to an expanding population of well over six billion souls, making unprecedented and still-increasing demands upon Earth's vital natural systems. As our numbers grow, the world's biosphere becomes subject to escalating ruin. Scientists now estimate that the extinction rate of animal and plant species, a primary indicator of overall global health, may be as much as hundreds of times the natural "background" rate in the fossil record.[7] Even though there have been at least five such mass extinction events in the geological past, these earlier episodes resulted from natural global climatic shifts or other catastrophes such as the colossal meteor impact that likely killed off the dinosaurs some sixty-five million years ago. For the first time, a spike in the species extinction rate is now occurring due to the activities of one of Earth's own biological creatures ... *Homo sapiens.*

Life in general suffers from humanity's dominion in virtually every part of the globe. Tropical rainforests such as the one I walked through as a young man with my wife disappear at a rate estimated between 45,000 and 60,000 square miles each year,[8] an area greater than all of Guatemala. Oceanic systems are in general decline, with many major fisheries showing clear signs of overexploitation,[9] and about one-quarter of the world's coral reefs are already dead.[10] Freshwater supplies that we rely on both for drinking and for food production are progressively degrading over much of the planet, particularly in South Asia.[11] Soil depletion has already reduced the world's cropland by one-third.[12] There is now a "dead zone" in the Gulf of Mexico equal to the size of New Jersey as a result of agricultural runoff,[13] and the BP oil leak now threatens to do serious harm to the many areas where the marine life has survived. Since 1900, we have lost three-fourths of the genetic diversity in our food crops through shortsighted agricultural practices.[14] Unfortunately, our damage to the natural world is surely even worse than such sobering statistics suggest since our perception of the limitless complexity inherent in biological systems is so narrow that we witness only the most obvious results of our destruction.

In the industrialized world, particularly in the United States, this worsening environmental crisis parallels a recent decline in the overall quality of daily human life. Responding to unchecked evolutionarily derived survival impulses within a context of ready availability, we increasingly eat a grossly inappropriate diet based on high percentages of saturated fats and refined carbohydrates. Instead of water, our primary liquid intake often takes the form of soft drinks—blends of artificial chemicals, superconcentrated sweeteners, tap water, and caffeine that compromise our health with every sip. Our preference for fast food, in combination with the effects of our ever-more-sedentary lifestyle, literally immobilizes us as obesity rises to levels that only decades ago would have been unimaginable. Tragically, millions of our children gain weight right along with us. Fundamental human activities like running and climbing are now difficult or impossible for many.

Artificial chemical additives and residues from agricultural toxins contaminate even much of the supposedly healthy food we consume. We regularly expose ourselves to thousands of agricultural agents, preservatives, and industrial by-products that our ancient evolutionary heritage has not prepared our bodies to process effectively. Not surprisingly, scientists have shown the presence of dozens of these toxins stored in our fatty tissue.[15] We have reached the point now when substantial levels of toxicity even contaminate human breast milk.[16]

Not surprisingly, our self-destructive diet, largely sedentary lifestyle, and polluted environment often lead to degenerative illnesses. In response, we attempt to medicate ourselves, heeding the advice of trusted health professionals and the rapidly multiplying pharmaceutical ads on television. Consumers in the United States alone fill more than three billion pharmaceutical prescriptions annually[17] and ingest more legal drugs than the rest of the world combined.[18] We do so while ignoring that nearly twice as many people in the United States die each year from unexpected prescription drug reactions than died in the entirety of the Vietnam War.[19] Perhaps most tellingly, prescriptions for children in the United States now rival those for senior citizens, with uncounted millions of children going off to school on mind-altering prescription drugs that are now distributed as a matter of routine.[20] The consumption of pharmaceuticals has become so rampant that there are now serious concerns about the effects of these drugs on the environment via human waste.

When our children come home from the classroom, they sit in front of a television set, on average, for more than four hours per day,[21] regularly "enjoying" thousands of deliberately manipulative advertisements convincing them to buy items that, more often than not, further the degeneration of the environment and their own bodies. Too busy from working to pay for these purchases, dedicated parents have less time left for the family, leaving their babies at daycare centers and consigning elders to nursing homes while our teens commit suicide at increasing rates. Excessive stress levels lead us into self-destructive consumption of alcohol, tobacco, both legal and illegal drugs, and numbing quantities of food.

Our religious traditions, which we naturally turn to in hopes of finding wise guidance, instead mirror our collective shortsightedness. Some espouse notions of God that at times border on sacrilegious parody, doing little to enable development of an integrated, experiential awareness of the divine such as that experienced by many Maya. Instead of pursuing the ageless wisdom of the world's sages, we feel convinced that if we can just be safe from our adversaries, acquire the necessary material goods, figure out the ideal combination of medications, and spend our time properly entertained, we will then finally be able to experience true happiness. To our dismay, as we fulfill our desires, the heartfelt experience of joy becomes as endangered as the animal and plant species struggling around the world for survival.

Given this overwhelmingly dire situation, we might expect a general clamor for radical and positive transformation. Instead, we have normalized our collective confusion to such an extent that we unquestioningly promote many myopic behaviors. We expend massive amounts of medical resources on better ways to detect and treat cancer while doing little to halt the release of countless carcinogens into the biosphere where we live. In a similarly self-defeating approach, as our freshwater supplies dwindle, we pour increasing amounts of the precious liquid on unnecessary lawns and exotic landscaping instead of simply using native vegetation already adapted to local ecosystems. We pay highly skilled medical professionals to cut open the human chest cavity with an electric saw in order to replace congested heart components at tremendous personal and societal expense while the preventative approach of eating a sensible diet and thus entirely avoiding the need for such a debilitating and costly procedure is viewed as exceedingly "alternative."[22] In spite of abundant signals calling us to stir from our collective slumber, in general, we remain tragically uninformed concerning our own bodies, the constraints we have placed on human potential, and the severity of our current global predicament. Ironically, apart from concerns over temporary downswings in the economy, our unspoken assumption is that we are currently experiencing the pinnacle of human achievement on planet Earth and that modern society embodies the finest expression of our species' potential as the ultimate provider of material well-being. Although humans have indeed made great advances, we seem blind to our self-destructive tendencies as we "trash" the living planet on which we depend so dearly.

Much as Classic Mayan civilization's spectacular success ultimately led to its calamitous collapse more than a thousand years ago, our own impressive achievements have led to this sorry state of affairs. Our society's technological sophistication and its capacity to enhance material well-being are unrivaled in human history. Yet, modern global society has excelled within a narrow trajectory of potential human development that has left us with our brain's evolutionary heritage underactivated and our consciousness stunted. Development of our beings has always been contingent upon direct interaction with the varied ecosystems of planet Earth. For millions of years, we ran after game, climbed high into trees, tended our crops, and slept on the ground, essentially living our lives outdoors. As our current lifestyle isolates us progressively more from the living planet, vital portions of our awareness either do not develop or they atrophy through disuse, much as the musculature of our bodies atrophies when denied exercise. States of human consciousness that developed through a continuous and interdependent relationship with nature are now also going extinct as the vital experiential bond between humans and nature becomes ever more tenuous.

Ironically, at first glance, when we in the developed world compare ourselves to Maya, on almost all of our customary scales of measurement, these native people come up lacking. For most rural Maya, income per capita is probably well under a thousand dollars per year and the physical demands of the typical workday are often extreme. Many people live in one-room adobe or stick structures with a dirt floor, no heating or air-conditioning, and a small fire for cooking. Rural families typically have no televisions, cars, refrigerators, computers, cooking appliances, washing machines, or CD players. Many Maya have no access to health care at all, much less health insurance. In short, Maya often lack what we in the modern lifestyle often consider as basic to our comfort and happiness.

In spite of the numerous difficulties faced by Maya, any person familiar with both their society and our own observes that, in general, Maya seem far more appreciative of and fulfilled with their lives than we do. If it were somehow possible to imagine the most truly representative Mayan person and a truly average Westerner, the average Maya would have numerous disadvantages in terms of creature comforts. Nevertheless, this prototypical Mayan figure would outshine the Western one in terms of basic psychological well-being. Some Maya are awake to aspects of the human experience that many of us are no longer even aware exist. The possibility that subsistence corn farmers could derive more satisfaction from their lives than we do challenges our deepest societal assumptions about what it means to lead a successful life and makes it prudent to consider the possibility that these "people of corn" have something to teach us.

The Era of 2012, a Time for Reflection

As Mayan friends familiar with 2012 have reminded me, the coming shift of 13 Pik affords humanity an opportunity for reflection and a chance to change direction on humanity's journey. The dire ecological and societal circumstances we have created now oblige us to act thoughtfully to avoid further irreparable damage to our home planet. We can and must transform ourselves and our societies; and the ideals of Mayan culture provide an experientially proven framework for beginning this radical renovation. The invaluable lessons from the living Maya are not esoteric messages from the stars or complex prophecies hidden in hieroglyphic texts that we must struggle to interpret. On the contrary, they are gems of wisdom drawn from thousands of years of human experience. They are the practical lessons in living that Mayan traditionalists have long held dear: cherish our babies, connect with our communities, revere the natural world that sustains us, seek the wisdom of humanity's elders, and immerse ourselves in direct experience of this divine world that we inhabit.

The path we humans walk in the era of 2012 appears full of perils on all sides. Even so, we can proceed with genuine confidence, knowing that many Maya have trod down more treacherous roads than this one and have emerged whole of spirit. We each have unique gifts to carry along on our species' earthly journey and we will need them all if we are to reach our common destination as one. As we gather up our burdens to take to the road, I imagine lightly touching your hand, as many Maya do, allowing us to sense one another's state of being, and repeating the simple words of the first Mayan man I met more than thirty years ago on a slippery rainforest trail. *"Koxla,"* "Let's go."

In the closing section of the holy *Popol Vuh*, the ancient K'iche' lords urge their descendants to stick to the Green Road, the verdant path Mayan culture associates with life-giving vegetation, the tender sprouts of baby humans, the living World Tree, the *axis mundi* that unites the sacred earth below our feet with the fathomless heavens. Green is the road to the cosmic center, to our latent human heritage of genuine wisdom bestowed upon us by our collective evolutionary origins in the living world. The ancient lords offered this heartfelt prayer for their people, one that I in turn repeat for all the peoples of the world:

May there be no blame, obstacle, want, or misery;
let no deceiver come behind or before.
May they neither be snared nor wounded,
nor seduced, nor burned,
nor diverted below the road or above it.
May they neither fall over backward nor stumble;
keep them on the Green Road, the Green Path.[23]

As the Maya of Yucatán say, *"Xi'ik tech utzil." May it go well for you.*

Glossary

Ah: K'iche' day-name; *Ben* (Yukatek)

Ahaw: Lord; K'iche' day-name

ahbe': "person of the road" (Q'anjobal)

Ahmaq: K'iche' day-name; *Kib* (Yukatek)

Ahpub: K'iche' day-name; the culminating day of the ritual calendar; the Lord; the sun; *Ahaw*

ahq'ih; ahq'ihab (plural): spiritual guide; calendar priest; "he/she of the day" (K'iche')

amh: skirt (Mam)

Aq'abal: K'iche' day-name; *Akabal* (Yukatek)

atole: beverage made from corn and water

Bakal: bone; a Classic Period city-state

Bakal Ahaw: Lord of Bone

baktun: a period of 144,000 days, known by the ancient Maya as *pik*

Batz': K'iche' day-name; *Chuen* (Yukatek)

be: trail; road; one's road in life

Bix a bel?: How is your road? (Yukatek)

Chebi.: Take it slow. (Mam)

Ch-honta: thanks (Mam)

chman: grandfather; grandchild

chmanbah: Mayan priest (Mam)

Ch'ol: a Mayan language

cholq'ih: count of suns; the 260-day ritual calendar (K'iche')

Chorti: a Mayan language and group in Guatemala

chuh: sauna (Mam)

dueños: guardian lords (Spanish)

Dyos: Mayanization of Spanish *Dios*; God

Dzulo'ob: those of European ancestry (Yukatek)

E': K'iche' day-name; *Eb* (Yukatek)

haab: 365-day cycle; also a 360-day cycle of 18 *winik* for the ancient Maya; *tun* (Yukatek)

Hach Akyum: a principal Lacandon deity

Hach Winik: "true people" in Lacandon, a Mayan language and group in Mexico

Hun Ahaw: One Lord, First Father, Corn God, father of Hunahpú/Xbalanqué

Hunahpú: "One Blowgunner," counterpart of Xbalanqué

'ilaj monpan: "he attended the ceremony of the nurturing of the sprouts" (in ancient Mayan language)

Imox: K'iche' day-name; *Imix* (Yukatek)

Iq': K'iche' day-name; *Ik* (Yukatek)

I'x: K'iche' day-name; day of the jaguar; *I'x* (Yukatek)

Iximulew: "land of corn," Guatemala

Jakalteko: a Mayan language and group in Guatemala

K'abal Xok: queen of Classic Period Yaxchilan

Kame: K'iche' day-name; *Kimi* (Yukatek)

Kan: K'iche' day-name; *Chikchan* (Yukatek)

k'an: cramp (Mam)

K'ank'in: one of the Mayan months

K'at: K'iche' day-name; *Kan* (Yukatek)

k'atun: twenty 360 day haabs (7,200 days); *winikhaab* (in ancient Mayan language)

K'awil: a deity; living staff; "instrument of rule"

Kawoq: K'iche' day-name; *Kawaq* (Yukatek)

Kechwa: a language group in the South American Andes

Keh: K'iche' day-name; *Manik* (Yukatek)

K'iche': a Mayan language and group in Guatemala

k'in: day in the ancient Mayan language

K'in Ahaw: Lord Sun

K'inich Hanaab' Pakal: seventh-century Mayan king

Kixta tzalu.: Come over here. (Mam)

Koxla.: Let's go. (Ch'ol)

k'uh: body's core, in middle of abdomen (Mam)

k'uhul: the divine (in ancient Mayan language)

kuku: dove (Tenek)

K'uk'ulkan: mythical Plumed Serpent

Glossary

Lacandon (Hach Winik): a Mayan language and group in Mexico

Lakam Ha': "Big Water"

lita: corn-only tamale (Mam)

Lom Ha: place where the holy "speaking" cross was found

ma': no (Yukatek)

Ma'alob: Okay (Yukatek)

Macewal: a Yukatek group in Eastern Yucatán; Cruzo'ob (Yukatek)

Ma chim.: He's died. (Mam)

mam: ancestors; ancestral spirit; living community elders; grandfather; father

Mam: a Mayan language and group in Guatemala

max: spider monkeys (Ch'ol)

Maximón: Rilah Mam; a Tz'utuhil deity

milpa: corn garden (Spanish)

nchyal: my son (Mam)

Nim Ya: "Big Water"

nixtamal: swollen hominy-like grains of corn

No'h: K'iche' day-name; *K'aban* (Yukatek)

Nuhsama: Forgive me. (Mam)

Oken'ex: Come in. (Yukatek)

oxlahun pik: thirteenth *baktun*

oxlanh: thirteen (Jakalteko)

Paxil: the Split Place, site of the mythological fabrication of humanity

pik: 20 *k'atun;* 144,000 days

pop: reed mat

Popol Vuh: "Book of the Council Mat," a sacred text

pox: remedy, medicine, cane sugar liquor (Tzotzil)

Q'anhobal: a Mayan language and group

Q'anil: K'iche' day-name; *Lamat* (Yukatek)

Q'antz tq'aba.: Give me your hand. (Mam)

q'ili: a small parrot species (Tenek)

qman: our father (Mam)

Qmantxun: "the limestone of our fathers" (Mam)

Rilaj Mam: a shape-changing deity; "Ancient Ancestor" (Tz'utuhil)

saq be': white/clear road

tahbal: headstrap (Ch'ol)

tat: sir; man (in many Mayan languages)

tata: father, grandfather (in many Mayan languages)

Tata K'icha: Grandfather Sun (Tenek)

Tenek: a Mayan language and group; *Huastec* in Spanish

teosinte: a wild grain plant that was the source of domestic corn

tey: you (Mam)

Ti ma txi?: Where are you going? (Mam)

tih: ancient ones (Mam)

tih xhal: ancient people (Mam)

Tihax: K'iche' day-name; *Etznab* (Yukatek)

Toh: K'iche' day-name; *Muluk* (Yukatek)

tuh: sauna (K'iche')

tun: a cycle of 360 days

Tx'otx': Earth (Mam)

Tzeltal: a Mayan language and group in Mexico

tzolkin: two-hundred and sixty-day ritual calendar

Tz'i: K'iche' day-name; *Ok* (Yukatek)

Tz'ikin: K'iche' day-name; *Men* (Yukatek)

tz'ite: *Erythrina corallodendron*

Tzotzil: a Mayan language and group in Mexico

Tz'ulo'ob: alternate spelling of *Dzulo'ob*; those of European ancestry (Yukatek)

Tz'utuhil: a Mayan language and group in Guatemala

Uxte'tun: city of Calakmul

vara: sacred staff; bundle of holy *tz'ite* seeds (Spanish)

wabh: tortilla; food (Mam)

winaq: person (K'iche')

winik: twenty *k'in*; twenty days

Xbalanqué: "Jaguar Deer," counterpart of Hunahpú

xhaw: the moon; "female lord" (Mam)

Xibalba: the underworld

Xi'ik tech utzil.: May it go well for you. (Yukatek)

Xmukane: female creator, "Grandmother of Day, Grandmother of Light"

Glossary

Xpiyakok: male creator

xu'tan: end-of-the-world tradition among Lacandon yax: blue (above)/green (below)

Yax Mutal: city of Tikal in Guatemala

yax te': kapok (ceiba) tree (Yukatek)

Yax Te': green vertical axis at the center of ancient Mayan cosmology

Yaxchilan: an ancient Mayan city

Yukatek: a Mayan language and group in Mexico and Belize

Notes

Acknowledgments to the Living Maya

1. With minor exceptions, the spelling of terms in Mayan languages in this book uses the conventions of the Guatemalan Academy of Mayan Languages. In this system, the /x/ sounds like the /sh/ sound in English except that the sound is produced with the tongue pointing slightly backward. An apostrophe after a letter indicates a glottal stop like that found in the middle of the English expression of concern, "uh oh." The /b'/ in Mayan languages is a glottal phoneme that sounds harder than the English /b/, but the simple /b/ appears in this book in Mayan words instead of the official spelling for the sake of simplicity. Another exceptional spelling is the /j/ sound in the official Guatemalan alphabet, which is represented here with an /h/ reflecting its approximate pronunciation in English.

Foreword by Patricio Balona

1. Yukatek Mayan term referring to those of European ancestry.

Chapter 1

1. The term "Maya" can be inadvertently misleading since it does not adequately reflect their world's extreme cultural diversity. There are some thirty Mayan languages, each with its own distinctive culture. Even within a single Mayan language group, there is sometimes substantial linguistic and cultural variability. The word "Maya" can refer specifically to the indigenous people of the Yucatán Peninsula, but most researchers commonly use the term to refer to all Native Americans in the region who partake of a broadly related cultural heritage. The word "Maya" may be more meaningful when referring to the ancient Maya since there appears to have been greater homogeneity in the Mayan world during the Classic Period (250–900 CE).

2. For those acquainted with scholarly debate concerning the correlation between our Gregorian calendar and the Mayan Long Count, I prefer the

Notes

584283 GMT (Goodman, Martinez, Thompson correlation) calculation since it produces the anticipated *baktun*-completing *tzolkin* date of 4 Ahaw on December 21, 2012, coinciding perfectly with the count of contemporary daykeeping Mayan priests in the Guatemalan highlands. *Pik* was the ancient Mayan term for what most now call a *baktun*, a period of 144,000 days in the Long Count. The 584283 GMT correlation places the start date of the 13 Pik cycle on a solar zenith passage at the latitude where the Long Count was likely invented, and establishes the end date on a winter solstice—an absolutely astounding mathematical and astronomical accomplishment and one impossible for me to dismiss as mere coincidence. In any case, the precise date for commemorating completion of this calendar cycle has no real significance for the purposes of this book.

3. *Ceiba pentandra.*

4. Better known in its Spanish spelling, Quechua.

5. www.livescience.com/environment/070910_pollution_deaths.html.

6. www.livescience.com/environment/070910_pollution_deaths.html

7. I cannot resist pointing out that most Americans are literally people made from corn due to our inordinate consumption of corn-derived sweeteners, corn oil, and corn-fed animals. Maya are also people of corn since most of their daily food intake comes in the form of tamales, tortillas, and corn gruel.

8. Mam is a multivalent term that I use here to refer to the revered Mayan "ancestors." The term also refers to a major Mayan language spoken by hundreds of thousands of people, primarily in western Guatemala. The Tz'utuhil Maya use the term to refer to Maximón, the shape-changing Mayan deity revered around Lake Atitlán. The Q'anhobal Maya use a variant of the term as a respectful form of address with adult males.

9. The term was coined in "The 2012 Phenomenon: New Age Appropriation of an Ancient Mayan Calendar," *Nova Religio* 9, no. 3 (February 2006).

10. Monument 6 from Tortuguero, Mexico, uses the term "13 Pik" and is the only known explicit ancient reference to the date. The term "13 Pik" also appears in Munro Edmonson's version of the *Chilam Balam of Chumayel*, p. 159, but the context is unclear.

11. Using the 584283 GMT correlation.

12. *Heaven Born Merida and Its Destiny: The Book of Chilam Balam of Chumayel,* trans. Munro S. Edmonson (Austin: University of Texas Press, 1986), 159.
13. Translation from the original hieroglyphic writing by Professor David Stuart.
14. Notable exceptions include the writings of Victor Montejo and José Mucía Batz (see www2.stetson.edu/~rsitler/13PIK/).
15. Esoteric Mayan religious texts from colonial period Yucatán.
16. Search performed on December 15, 2009.
17. This conclusion is based on a review of the relevant literature and informal investigation in various communities in more than a dozen different Mayan linguistic groups plus interviews with dozens of Mayan spiritual guides and religious officials.
18. Maud Worcester Makemson, *The Book of the Jaguar Priest: A Translation of the Book of Chilam Balam of Tizimin* (New York: Henry Schuman, 1951), 30, n. 92.
19. Anthony Aveni, *The End of Time: The Maya Mystery of 2012* (Boulder, CO: University Press of Colorado, 2009), 164.
20. José Argüelles, *The Mayan Factor: Path Beyond Technology* (Santa Fe, NM: Bear & Co., 1987), 159.
21. Argüelles, *The Mayan Factor,* 20.
22. José Argüelles, "José Speaks Out," www.earthportals.com/Portal_Messenger/speakout.html (accessed January 20, 2009).
23. José Argüelles, FAQ, www.13moon.com/time-is-art.htm (accessed January 20, 2009).
24. José Argüelles, www.2013.net/multidim/mayas/time/tattvan.txt (accessed January 20, 2009).
25. www.lawoftime.org/home.html (accessed December 16, 2009).
26. José Argüelles, www.realitysandwich.com/2012_now_everybodys_mind (accessed December 15, 2009).
27. The celestial alignment itself is an annual event but its occurrence on the Northern Hemisphere winter solstice takes place at intervals of approximately 25,800 years
28. John Major Jenkins, *Maya Cosmogenesis 2012* (Santa Fe, NM: Bear & Co., 1998), 159.
29. Personal communication, December 2009.

30. Aveni, *The End of Time*, 54.

31. Steven McFadden, *Profiles in Wisdom* (Santa Fe, NM: Bear & Co., 1991), 229.

32. He is also known widely as Don Alejandro, especially outside of Guatemala.

33. Personal communication with Elizabeth Araujo, October 2006

34. www.youtube.com/watch?v=y9wfenrHU-I&feature=PlayList&p=659764DEB2893981&index=0.

35. This is a reference to the contemporary descendants of the rebel Mayan forces during the Caste War in the late nineteenth century. Some scholars also refer to them as Cruzo'ob', "those of the Cross."

36. Paul Sullivan, *Unfinished Conversations: Mayas and Foreigners Between Two Wars* (New York: Alfred A. Knopf, 1989), 162.

37. Jesús J. Lizama Quijano, "Las señales del fin del mundo: Una aproximación a la tradición profética de los cruzo'ob" ("Signs of the End of the World: An Approach to the Prophetic Tradition of the Cruzo'ob") at www.mayas.uady.mx/articulos/tradicion.html (accessed January 20, 2009). My translation from the original Spanish.

38. Nelson A. Reed, *The Caste War of Yucatán* (Stanford: Stanford University Press, 2001), 343–44.

39. Personal communication with Patricio Balona, December 2009.

40. Victor Perera and Robert D. Bruce, *The Last Lords of Palenque: The Lacandon Mayas of the Mexican Rain Forest* (Boston: Little, Brown & Co., 1982), 49. Hach Akyum (my spelling) is the primary Lacandon deity.

41. Patricio Balona provided this summary of our chat in Lacanjá Chansayab.

42. All references to *tat* Rigoberto Itzep Chanchavac arose in personal conversations at our respective homes and through email.

43. Four of the twenty day-names are year-bearers. A *haab* (365-day year) always begins on one of these four days. The year-bearer's influence is felt throughout each of these particular four periods.

44. Personal conversation, August 2006.

45. Tape-recorded conversation with Gaspar González on December 27, 1996.

46. http://www2.stetson.edu/~rsitler/perspectives/

47. Gaspar Pedro González, *El 13 Baktun: La nueva era 2012*, self-published, 2006.

48. Gaspar González, *13 Baktun: Mayan Visions of 2012 and Beyond* (Berkeley, CA: North Atlantic Books, 2010).

49. Victor Montejo, *Maya Intellectual Renaissance: Identity, Representation, and Leadership* (Austin: University of Texas Press, 2005), 120–122.

50. Personal message, December 2009.

51. According to Edward Cleary, Protestant denominations make up about 25 percent of the total population in Guatemala. Cleary, "Shopping Around: Questions About Latin American Conversions," *International Bulletin of Missionary Research* (April 2004), www.providence.edu/las/Brookings.html (accessed September 8, 2005). This figure may be much higher for the Maya alone.

52. In Todos Santos Cuchumatán, belief in a coming *fin del mundo* ("end of the world") is commonplace among those belonging to the town's three principal fundamentalist churches.

Chapter 2

1. This magnificent archaeological site is near the modern Mexican town of Palenque in the state of Chiapas.

2. Pronounced like a long *E* in English, cut off abruptly at the end.

3. A term used by the K'iche' Mayan people of Guatemala.

4. Pronounced roughly like "bay" in English.

5. In K'iche' Maya.

6. This trail is now closed to the public.

Chapter 3

1. Rigoberta Menchú, *I, Rigoberta Menchú: An Indian Woman in Guatemala* (London: Verso, 1984), 7–8.

2. *Popol Vuh: The Definitive Edition of the Mayan Book of the Dawn of Life and the Glories of Gods and Kings*, trans. Dennis Tedlock (New York: Touchstone, 1996), 69.

3. June Sitler, January 2010.

Notes

Chapter 4

1. Perera and Bruce, *The Last Lords of Palenque.*
2. Robert D. Bruce, *Lacandon Dream Symbolism* (Mexico, D.F.: Ediciones Euroamericanas, 1975), 110–11.

Chapter 5

1. *Popol Vuh,* 110.
2. Literally, "he/she of the day," a K'iche' word for Mayan calendar priest.
3. http://nawalwinaq.blogspot.com/ (accessed January 7, 2010).
4. Personal communication, January 2010.
5. Raymond Stadelman, *Maize Cultivation in Northwestern Guatemala* (Washington: Carnegie Institute, 1940).

Chapter 6

1. A word in the Mam language that refers both to "grandfathers" and "grandchildren."

Chapter 7

1. Gaspar Pedro González, *A Mayan Life* (Rancho Palos Verdes, CA: Yax Te', 1995), 88.
2. González, *A Mayan Life,* 90.
3. Bruce, *Lacandon Dream Symbolism,* 39.
4. Reed, *The Caste War of Yucatán,* 141.
5. Reed, *The Caste War of Yucatán,* 185.
6. Barbara Tedlock, *Time and the Highland Maya* (Albuquerque: University of New Mexico Press, 1992), 189–90.
7. Brian Stross, "Maize and Fish: The Iconography of Power in Late Formative Mesoamerica," *Res: Anthropology and Aesthetics* 25 (1994): 29–31.
8. Prudence M. Rice, *Maya Calendar Origins: Monuments, Mythistory, and the Materialization of Time* (Austin: University of Texas Press, 2007).

Chapter 8

1. There were several other writing systems that emerged in Mesoamerica but none came near to the complexity or broad usage of the Mayan script.
2. Robert J. Sharer, *The Ancient Maya*, 6th ed. (Stanford: Stanford University Press., 2006), 513.
3. Reed, *The Caste War of Yucatán*, 141.
4. John Lloyd Stephens, *Incidents of Travel in Yucatan* (Washington, DC: Smithsonian Institution Press, 1996).
5. Reed, *The Caste War of Yucatán*, 122.
6. Raxche' (Demetrio Rodríguez Guaján), "Maya Culture and the Politics of Development," in Edward F. Fischer and R. McKenna Brown, *Maya Cultural Activism in Guatemala* (Austin: University of Texas Press, 1996), 80.
7. www.msnbc.msn.com/id/6502368/.
8. www.wri.org/wri/trends/deforest.html.
9. www.wri.org/wri/trends/fishloss.html.
10. www.aims.gov.au/pages/research/coral-bleaching/scr2000/scr-00gcrmn -report.html.
11. http://unesdoc.unesco.org/images/0012/001295/129556e.pdf.
12. www.wri.org/wri/trends/soilloss.html.
13. www.sciencedaily.com/releases/2009/06/090618124956.htm.
14. www.fao.org/docrep/U8480E/U8480E0k.htm.
15. http://www.orionmagazine.org/index.php/articles/article/133/
16. http://healthandenergy.com/toxic_breast_milk.htm
17. http://www.statehealthfacts.org/profileind.jsp?sub=66&rgn=1&cat=5
18. James Gorman, "The Altered Human Is Already Here," *New York Times*, April 6, 2004.
19. www.mercola.com/2003/nov/26/death_by_medicine.htm.
20. www.salon.com/health/feature/2000/03/09/kid_drugs.
21. www.designshare.com/Research/Orr/Loving_Children.htm.
22. Stetson University American Studies Professor Paul Croce's comment from a personal conversation.
23. *Popol Vuh*, 193.

About the Author

ROBERT K. SITLER, PHD, serves as Director of Stetson University's Latin American Studies Program in DeLand, Florida, where he also teaches courses in Spanish, Mayan culture, and Latin American humanities. He has spent significant time among speakers of ten different Maya languages, spanning a period of more than thirty years. He studied with the late Mayan scholar Dr. Linda Schele while working on his doctoral dissertation at the University of Texas at Austin in 1994. The author of many articles on the Maya, Dr. Sitler has focused his recent work on the developing social phenomenon surrounding the 2012 date in the Mayan Long Count calendar. His unique perspective is in part due to a spiritual experience in Palenque, Mexico, that greatly influences his life and writing. More information on him can be found at www.robertsitler.com.